THE BIRMINGHAM NAVIGATIONS

Volume 1 1768–1846

by

S. R. BROADBRIDGE

With plates and maps

DAVID & CHARLES : NEWTON ABBOT

0 7153 6381 6

© S. R. Broadbridge 1974

All rights reserved. No part of this publication may be reproduced, stored in a retrieval system, or transmitted, in any form or by any means, electronic, mechanical, photocopying, recording or otherwise, without the prior permission of David & Charles (Holdings) Limited

Set in 11pt Garamond, 2pt leaded
and printed in Great Britain
by Latimer Trend & Company Ltd Plymouth
for David & Charles (Holdings) Limited
South Devon House   Newton Abbot   Devon

£1·75

THE BIRMINGHAM CANAL NAVIGATIONS
VOL 1
1768–1846

INLAND WATERWAYS HISTORIES
Edited by Charles Hadfield

The Ballinamore & Ballyconnell Canal. By Patrick Flanagan
The Birmingham Canal Navigations, Vol I. By S. R. Broadbridge
The Bude Canal. By Helen Harris and Monica Ellis
The Dorset & Somerset Canal. By Kenneth R. Clew
The Grand Canal of Ireland. By Ruth Delany
The Grand Junction Canal. By Alan H. Faulkner
The Grand Western Canal. By Helen Harris
The Great Ouse. By Dorothy Summers
The Kennet & Avon Canal. By Kenneth R. Clew
The Leicester Line. By Philip A. Stevens
London's Lost Route to Basingstoke. By P. A. L. Vine
London's Lost Route to the Sea. By P. A. L. Vine
The Nutbrook Canal. By Peter Stevenson
The Royal Military Canal. By P. A. L. Vine
The Somersetshire Coal Canal and Railways. By Kenneth R. Clew
The Thames & Severn Canal. By Humphrey Household
The Yorkshire Ouse. By Baron F. Duckham

in preparation

The Derby Canal. By Peter Stevenson
The Exeter Canal. By Kenneth R. Clew
The Forth & Clyde Canal. By Graham Matheson and D. Light
The Leicester Navigation. By Philip A. Stevens
The Manchester Ship Canal. By Edward Paget-Tomlinson
The Nene. By Ronald Russell
The Oxford Canal. By Hugh Compton
The Shropshire Union Canals. By H. Robinson
The Stroudwater Navigation. By M. A. Handford
The Warwick Canals. By Alan H. Faulkner

'The Birmingham Canal, with its immense Local Trade, with its numerous Branches traversing in every direction the richest and most enterprising Mineral District in the Kingdom, is without a parallel, & must be judged of solely, with reference to its own peculiar circumstances'
(General Assembly Minute Book of the BCN,
9 November 1838)

Contents

		page
	List of Illustrations	9
1	THE FIRST CANAL, 1768–72	11
2	RIVALRIES AND EXPANSION, 1772–85	29
3	NEW CANALS, 1790–1830	46
4	IMPROVING THE BIRMINGHAM CANAL, 1778–1818	74
5	TELFORD AND AFTER, 1818–47	98
6	CONTROL AND FINANCE	120
7	MAINTENANCE AND OPERATION	144
8	THE COMING OF THE RAILWAYS	169
	Notes	187
	Acknowledgements	198
	Index	199

List of Illustrations

PLATES	page
Navigation Office, Paradise Street	49
Gas Street Basin	49
Spon Lane top lock	50
Farmer's Bridge	50
Lock, Farmer's Bridge	67
East End of Lappal Tunnel	67
Smethwick locks	68
Three canal levels, Smethwick	68
Horse boat at Spon Lane locks	149
Day Boat at Perry Barr locks	149
Lamp standard, Farmer's Bridge	150
Riders Green locks	150
Blowers Green Junction	167
Buildings over side pounds, Farmer's Bridge locks	167
Toll-office on Bentley Canal	168
Locks on Bentley Canal	168

LIST OF ILLUSTRATIONS

MAPS AND ILLUSTRATIONS IN THE TEXT

		page
1	Map of First Canal, 1772	27
2	Map of Extensions to 1815	96
3	Factory on Canal, 1827	110
4	Salford Junction, c 1855	114
5	Tame Valley Canal, c 1855	115
6	Map of Developments, 1815–47	118
7	Diagram of profits, dividends and share prices, 1770–1845	129
8	Advertisement for fly-boats, 1837	179

TABLES

1	The controlling Group of the Birmingham Canal	122
2	Profit and Loss Accounts at Quinquennial Intervals for the Birmingham Canal	132
3	Consolidated Profit and Loss Accounts for the Birmingham Canal, 1767–1800, 1801–25 and 1826–40	134

CHAPTER 1

The First Canal 1768-72

BIRMINGHAM is far from ideally situated to be the centre of a canal network, located as it is on the top of a plateau with steep slopes in all directions and a high ridge along the centre. Yet it was this that made the canals essential, since the main roads avoided the gradients and the rivers were too swift-flowing for transport, even had they not been used as sources of power. Nevertheless, the difficulties were great; as the system finally took shape there were three main levels, the Walsall (408ft OD), the Birmingham (453ft) and the Wolverhampton (473ft), linked by locks. A loop in the main ridge necessitated five major tunnels on the plateau and several deep cuttings and at the edges of the plateau the canals were forced to descend by steep flights of locks in order to connect with the rest of the system.

The town of Birmingham and its immediate neighbourhood are contrasted geologically with the Black Country and this soon led to a division of function whereby coal and iron were produced in the Black Country and worked up in Birmingham. By the middle of the eighteenth century the manufacture of brass had been added and the town was a thriving centre of industry with a wide diversification of trades, of which iron-working was the chief:

> The famous Old Square, in which dwelt so many of the notabilities of the town at one time or another, was itself the creation of an ironmaster, John Pemberton. Abraham and Isaac Spooner, Randle Bradburn, Charles and Sampson Lloyd, Samuel Garbett—all iron masters or merchants—had houses here; and the Square became the fashionable centre to which gravitated prosperous iron masters

who desired to transmute their wealth into social prestige—Richard Baddeley who owned a furnace at Rushall, Richard Parkes of Wednesbury, his partner John Fidoe, William and Harry Hunt, who conducted the slitting mill at Halesowen, and Samuel Garbett, who claimed to be the largest importer of Swedish bar iron, outside London.[1]

The industrial development of which this wealth was a symptom, only aggravated the transport problem, and it is no accident that many of the names listed above will reappear later in this history.

Before the 1760s the only outlets to wider markets were via the Trent, officially navigable to Burton, but between there and Shardlow 'greatly obstructed by Floods in Winter, and by the Shallows in Summer, so as to render the Carriage of Goods upon it uncertain and precarious',[2] and the Severn, navigable to Bewdley. A cursory glance at *Aris's Birmingham Gazette* at that date shows abundance of advertisements from wharfingers and carriers on both rivers soliciting custom.[3]

At that date, too, came the first beginnings of that skeleton of a national system of canals planned by Brindley and by him called 'The Cross'. The Trent & Mersey Canal was begun in 1766 and provoked the question, based on an estimate of necessary and proposed tonnages 'Whether it is equitable to fix a Tax upon a Commerce between this Neighbourhood and Gainsborough . . . to favour a Navigation between Shugborough and the River Mersey?'[4] It was planned to link it to the Severn by a canal (the Staffs & Worcs) from Shugborough (later Great Haywood) and to the Thames by two canals (the Coventry and the Oxford) from Fradley to Coventry and from the latter to Oxford. All of these canals carefully skirted round the Birmingham plateau, that to the Severn reaching nearest at the bottom of a steep rise to Wolverhampton. As a result the long pack-horse trails were shortened but this advantage was cancelled by the great access to coalfields and markets gained by rival ironworking areas.

A reliable route by which coal could be brought to Birmingham

THE FIRST CANAL, 1768–72

therefore became the prime need if prosperity was to be retained. In January 1767 one of *Aris's* correspondents inquired if it would 'not be an acceptable Service, if any one could point out a plan, which if steadily pursued, might in Time Remedy the Evil' of the appalling state of the 'Road to the Coal-pits'.[5] This emphasis on the inward traffic was always to be found amongst the canal's promoters, though through the application of the Staffs & Worcs Canal (so it was alleged) they were 'induced to petition Parliament for a continuance of their Canal Six or Seven Miles further . . . to communicate with their Canal at Autherley'.[6] Be that as it may, there was not lacking 'A Well wisher to the Town' with a suggestion of 'a Navigable Cut from Wolverhampton Canal, through the Coal Works, to this town'[7] as a solution to all difficulties. He stated that the amount of coal carried annually to Birmingham was 72,800 tons at a transport cost of 5d per cwt, which could be reduced to 3¼d or 4¼d. Since he assumed that the canal could be built for £15,000 and had no running costs, there would be at worst nearly £7,000 available each year 'for the Support of the Poor'.

After this things moved rapidly. The next week, as a result of this letter, the constables, churchwardens, and overseers called a meeting for 28 January in the Swan Inn, at which it was agreed to ask James Brindley to prepare a plan and estimates. Thirty-five gentlemen, later increased by 130 others, in all a fair cross-representation of the town's trade and industry, agreed to pay a guinea each towards the cost, 'In Consequence of which Subscription, a Plan of the said intended Canal, as also, Two distinct and separate Estimates of the Expence thro' two different Courses or Channels, were taken.'[8]

Meanwhile other estimates were being made. One suggested that the canal would cost £20,000 and would sell 73,000 tons of coal yearly, purchased at 2d per cwt, for 4d per cwt, paying eighty boatmen 12s (60p) per week, six clerks £50 per annum and having the boats unloaded free by the workhouse poor. With interest at 5 per cent he calculated a profit of £8,371 of which £3,000 yearly would remain to pay off the principal after maintaining the town's poor. Any surplus above this could be 'converted to the Use of the Town in cleaning the Streets, and lighting the principal Part with Lamps'.[9]

Needless to say, the promoters of the canal had quite other ideas of what should be done with the profits, and this was to cause conflict later.[10]

Brindley produced his two plans at a meeting on 4 June and the 'Upper Way' was chosen, 'from near New-Hall, over Birmingham Heath, to or near the following places, viz. Smithwick, Oldbury, Tipton-Green, Bilston and from thence to the Staffordshire and Worcestershire Canal, with Branches to different Coal Works between the respective Places.'[11] The cost was not expected to exceed £50,000. At a meeting on 12 June to open a subscription a committee was elected of 39 members, of whom four—Samuel Garbett, Matthew Boulton, William Bentley and John Kettle—were to receive money. Within a month thirty landowners along the route had been approached and were unanimously in favour, £35,400 had been promised and a Parliamentary agent appointed.

By October matters were sufficiently advanced for a call of $2\frac{1}{2}$ per cent to be made on subscribers to pay the Parliamentary expenses. A general meeting on 13 November replaced the committee with one of nine members, five to be a quorum.[12]

It was at this time that the first shots were fired in a battle over the way in which the canal was to be conducted. A letter appeared in the press alleging that the public were being kept in the dark about the terms of the proposed Bill, 'and consequently . . . cannot tell if they are to be benefitted or not by that Scheme, which at first proposal was so much to serve the Town and Country'. The writer's main fear was that the probable extent of the coal trade had been underestimated to justify the proposed tonnage of $1\frac{1}{2}$d per ton-mile and he suggested 'that if a larger Quantity should come, the Tonnage ought to be so much reduced in Proportion, that the Subscribers should share no larger Dividends than if that was the exact Quantity.'[13]

Others were canvassing the idea of a limitation of dividends and a public meeting in December decided to petition against the Bill for a limit of 10 per cent, 'it being understood that the Calculation made of the Quantities . . . is vastly short, and consequently the Profits . . . will be thereby greatly heightened.' Supporters of the Bill wondered whether any of the critics would have ventured their own money under the restrictions suggested,

> and particularly if their Books and Papers were liable to be canvassed and inspected at the Discretion of the Curious, the Malignant or the Designing? an innovation of Power dreadful in all Countries, but particularly alarming to a free-born Englishman.

With superb logic it was both denied that the subscribers could even hope for a dividend as high as 6 per cent and argued that the proposed restriction should be opposed.[14]

The matter was raised with the committee by some proprietors who put proposals which would have made the proposed canal in some respects analogous to a turnpike trust. It was suggested that dividends should be limited to 10 per cent, the surplus being used to buy back shares, keep down tonnage rates, 'or for any other public purpose'. Up to £4,000 of the surplus could be invested in public funds to bring the dividend up to 5 per cent if repairs or other expenses reduced the profits to below this level. The accounts were to be inspected annually at a public meeting by commissioners appointed for the purpose.

In their reply the committee argued that the Bill was modelled on its predecessors,[15] that they did not expect as much as 6 per cent profit and 'that the Gentlemen have not duly considered the Evil that may be consequent upon a Number of Commissioners being invested with a power of inspecting the Accounts of any Company, and much more should that Power be extended in so unprecedented and absolute a manner as that proposed'. Finally, they claimed that if the proposals were included in the Bill it would be delayed for a year, whereby the subscribers would be put to expense and the town lose £8,000, which would 'in course be most severely felt by the poor'. Privately they decided to try to get the Bill through with no restriction, 'but if they are submitted to the alternative by Parliament of taking the Bill with the Restriction or losing it, to submit to the Restriction'.[16]

In the event the crucial amendment was rejected on 26 January and the Bill, having passed the Lords with no amendment, received the Royal Assent early in February.[17] Besides including matters more usually the subject of by-laws, it authorised the company to raise £55,000 in shares of £100, no one to have more than ten nor less than one share, with power to raise another £15,000 if necessary. There were three pages of listed commissioners (five to be a quorum) to settle disputes about land prices, with power to make the sheriff impanel a jury to enforce compulsory purchase. They were also to supervise tolls. The company's affairs were to be carried on by a committee of fifteen persons, each holding at least three shares.

The owners of mines could drain them into tunnels or aqueducts by soughs but must not dig within 12yd of the canal—though they could follow minerals under it in headings less than 6ft high and 4ft wide, a clause that was to cause trouble later. Millowners were protected by clauses laying it down that overflow weirs were to be made above all locks to feed mill-ponds 'and that the Water shall not be wilfully wasted by leaving open the said Locks longer than shall be necessary'.

Maximum tolls (later ruled to be also minima) were fixed at $1\frac{1}{2}$d per ton-mile, with road-metalling, dung, soil, marl and other manure going free provided they passed locks only 'at such Times when the Water shall flow over or through the Gauge Paddle or Ditch'. If the canal was not completed to the Staffs & Worcs Canal within 6 months of completion to Birmingham, then they should have power to complete it themselves and charge the company.

The Act once behind them the committee set down to work. Clay was sought for bricks, suppliers were requested for timber and barrows, Brindley was requested to send Henshall and Whitworth to resurvey the route and advertisements were issued for a head clerk or superintendent of works, an under clerk 'who must be a strong able Man, and perfectly versed in Measuration of all

Kinds' and for 'several Foremen or Undertakers, who perfectly understand the Nature of Navigation Business, and can bring with them a sufficient number of Workmen, to whom the Proprietors will let the Cutting of the Canal in Parcels'.[18]

The first annual general meeting was held on 25 March. Meredith, who had been acting as solicitor to the committee, was appointed clerk at a salary of £100pa, John Kettle as treasurer (upon entering into sureties for £5,000), Brindley as surveyor at £200pa and George Holloway as clerk-of-works at a salary of £100. William Wright was appointed under-clerk at £70pa and Joseph Dallaway book-keeping clerk at £50, thus completing a fairly substantial administrative set-up. Each proprietor was to have 3s 6d (17½p) per day expenses at general meetings, with a dinner allowance, and committee members 5s (25p) per day, Brindley was paid £120 back expenses and plate valued at £50 and £30 was voted to Messrs Bentley and Wilkinson. Provision having been thus made for past and future services a call of 10 per cent was made and the committee elected.

Brindley's original route had envisaged a tunnel at Smethwick. In June the committee went over the route in this section with him and having

> 'particularly examin'd and survey'd the course of the intended Tunnel . . . having bored and sunk several pits, and discovered running sand and other bad materials [Brindley] Gave it as his Opinion that the best way was to avoid tunnelling; and to carry the Canal over the Hills by Locks and Fire Engines'.[19]

The committee concurred and Simcock, who seems to have been resident engineer, was ordered to survey the proposed summit to find sources of water. Three weeks later he reported seven sources totalling '200¾ square inches'. Not surprisingly, the committee were mystified.

By October it could be said that the canal 'is in great forwardness; upwards of Five Miles is complete, and it is expected in a Year Goods will be sent from hence by means of this Canal to Bristol'.[20] However, the route in the Oldbury area was still undecided. Consideration was given to changing the course from the middle of the flight of six locks at Spon Lane so as to proceed on the upper side of Bilston in order to get a better supply of water and go through more coalmines. Brindley agreed on the new route and felt it was best to take it from the middle of the flight, the route that was finally adopted, but first Simcock was ordered to survey the same route both from there and from the summit. Later it was to be alleged that this new route was laid out, contrary to Brindley's advice, in order to avoid certain mines which were rivals to those owned by William Bentley, a leading member of the committee, in particular those of Found and Aston near Tipton. By this it was said that the company lost £40 weekly in tonnage. Samuel Garbett in particular charged that Brindley had '*a very sore Quarrel*' with Bentley over this matter since the original plan submitted to Parliament had shown 12 miles of canal from Spon Lane to Autherley and by January 1771 6 of these remained to be cut but the other 6 had grown to 12, none on the original line, presumably to avoid certain mines and to increase mileage receipts. In 1768, however, all this lay in the future, and construction proceeded on the new line.

As events turned out the canal was completed in three stages. The first was the section from the Wednesbury coal-fields to Birmingham, the second, completed only after considerable trouble and litigation, the two termini in Birmingham, and the third the section from Spon Lane to the Staffs & Worcs Canal.

By April 1769 water was already in part of the canal since boats were bought for use in further construction, and in the same month it claimed its first casualty, a man whose body was found floating near one of the Spon Lane locks. By October 'a sober diligent man, of unexceptional Character, who understands Accounts', was being sought, to be 'capable of undertaking the entire conduct of a Wharf at the Termination of the Canal', as were men to man boats and to 'attend at the Locks'.[21]

By the end of that month the public were informed 'that several Barges laden with Coals, are expected to come down the Canal next Week, Water being already let into a great Part of it'.

In fact, the first 'barges' arrived on 6 November and greatly reduced coal prices. Three days later it was reported:

> On Monday there arived by the Canal, at the temporary Wharf near this Town, three Boats, Yesterday three Boats, and three Boats are hourly expected, loaded with about 200 Tons of Coal; and the same are selling at the Wharf at fourpence Halfpenny per Hundred of 120 lb.[22]

Nevertheless waggons were still being used to bring in the coal, such was the demand, and to sell it at 7d or 8d until the traffic on the canal was able to increase.

> Sure that plan must be of noble use,
> That tends in price provision to reduce,

said a local poet, congratulating the company on their speedy exertions:

> Eighteen months have scarce run
> Since the work was begun . . .
> But for this good care and trouble
> That has nobly been display'd,
> For our coals, this instant, double
> What we give, we must have paid.
> Griping souls, that live by fleecing
> And upon their teams depend,
> To all ranks of life how pleasing
> That their day is at an end.

Not surprisingly, he concluded that 'the cut of all Cuts is a Birmingham Cut'.[23]

The coal came along the Wednesbury line but it was not taken all the way into Birmingham. As early as May 1769 a special General Assembly had considered the alternative routes into the town, accepted the one proposed by Simcock as far as Friday Street (now Summer Row) but deferred a final decision. In the meantime the committee purchased a piece of land at Brickkiln Piece (now Gas Street basin) and ordered Simcock to draw up plans for wharves. No construction was, however, undertaken, and the first coal was unloaded at Friday Street. At the other end the canal reached only to Spon Lane locks at Oldbury on the main line, but the company was bound to complete to a junction with the Staffs & Worcs Canal within six months of completion to Birmingham.

They were not entirely free to set their minds to these problems since they had internal troubles which, having smouldered underground for some time, now burst to view in the public press. Those who wished the canal to be built as a public service, who were now seen to include Samuel Garbett, had been waging a struggle in the committee which was not recorded in the minutes. As a result the sixth General Assembly was the scene of a lengthy debate which led to the decision, 'upon examining into the particulars of a Misunderstanding which has happen'd, in the Committee between Messieurs Garbett and Bentley,' that

> Mr. Garbett did not intend to insinuate Mr. Bentley's having wilfully mispent any of the Co's money . . . and (taking the whole of Mr. Bentley's conduct into Consideration) that the Public were under obligation to him—It likewise appeared that Mr. Garbett did frequently request for the Poor to be fully supply'd with Coal in preference to any Persons whatsoever and that there is no reason to say, that he ever did make a point for Mr. Turner's work to receive the Constant supply of Three Tons per day.[24]

At this time Garbett was alleging, privately, that the price of coal could be reduced to $3\frac{1}{2}$d per cwt of 120lb 'if a little Attention should be given to the Subject by Persons of Rank within this and the Neighbouring Counties',[25] but he seems to have felt that the time had come to make a public stand. He and Turner, his partner, therefore resigned from the committee, selling enough of their shares to disqualify themselves and issuing a printed statement to the proprietors. They stated that they had tried, but failed, to get standing orders 'with such apparent Equity as would satisfy the most Suspicious that Confusion was not designedly adopted to give opportunities for Artful Men to gain possession of private Jobbs unoticed'. They were therefore calling a Town's Meeting to consider a petition to Parliament to enforce this in order to prevent private views prevailing over public ones.

The petition which they drew up said that the canal might prejudice long-established manufacturers, since the company itself traded in coal and 'possessed themselves of the most convenient Landing Places for Wharfs and Warehouses'. It reiterated their belief in the possibility of a canal which, paying 4 per cent interest, could repay its capital in twenty or thirty years and then be free of tolls, with coal consequently a third cheaper.[26]

Once the first shots had been fired, battle became general, and both sides wrote freely to the press, the main attack being developed against Bentley: 'one of the Committee, and who is most principally concerned in the Direction, hath . . . a Share in some Coal Works and may order the Canal for his own private Advantage, to the Loss of the Company.'[27]

A lull in this verbal warfare ensued in the spring, but some coalowners still harboured resentment and clearly made statements that have not come down to us. In May, for example, Meredith was ordered to write to one of them 'to know what he meant by saying he could open such a scene of iniquity as could surprize the Cttee',[28] but opposition again became vocal in August when a new canal was proposed to run from the Trent & Mersey Canal near Lichfield to Wednesbury. In November another canal to Wednesbury was being surveyed from the Coventry Canal, with a branch to Birmingham. Soon the press was filled with letters which made it clear why these plans were receiving support:

> It is apprehended that the present Navigation from the Coal Pits to Birmingham is an improper Line for the *General Interest* of the Country, and to *prevent Monopolies*, and an *unnecessary* Tax upon Coals, that it is necessary to make another Canal.[29]

The efforts of others, however, were devoted to trying 'to obtain a *Free Navigation and a proper Use of the Banks*, on the Birmingham Canal, together with free Access thereto', and in December Garbett planned to lay before a Town's Meeting what he had found of the company's misdeeds, stating in the advertisement that '*It has been represented* that their proceedings have been arbitrary and oppressive, *and that*, having the Power, they have also shown the Inclination, to establish a dangerous Monopoly'. It was proposed that wharves should be owned by the parish, with storage space for all dealers, and that the company's coal trade should be regulated to prevent 'their showing Partiality to their own Connections and Interest'. It was now that the matter of the change of route was raised, but unfortunately the public controversy was suddenly silenced since *Aris*, 'having received from his distant Friends' (as he put it) 'Variety of Complaints, that his Paper is filled with Disputes relative to the Birmingham Navigation', summarily closed the correspondence.[30]

A petition from the coal owners was sent to the Commons while they were considering the matter of the canal's terminus, reiterating many of the grievances, 'and that the said Company are enabled to exercise Partiality to Proprietors of Land and of Coal in many important Instances, and to form a dangerous Monopoly,[31] but their pleas were ignored in the resulting Act. Garbett, however, told the General Assembly in March that he intended to go to Parliament in a few days to proceed upon a petition, but nothing seems to have been done. It would seem probable that the successful conclusion of the matter of the terminus, together with resulting changes in the committee (from which Bentley was removed) and the growth of competition in the coal trade, removed the main causes of grievance.

Trouble about the terminus at the Birmingham end had begun in October 1769, when the fifth General Assembly decided that the company would set up its own wharves where convenient, prevent anything being unloaded elsewhere and forbid landowners to erect wharves themselves—measures which would seem to go some way towards justifying the charges made against the company of attempting to create a monopoly. They further decided that they were not compelled by law to continue to New Hall Ring; it was therefore agreed to postpone further discussion about the price to be offered for the land, which belonged to William Colmore, and to take the advice of 'one or two able Counsel'. Colmore was not slow to reply and in December made it clear that he 'expect[ed] and require[d] that you do forthwith Proceed to compleat and finish with all convenient Speed your Canal to the field called New Hall Ring,' offering his land at £4 per acre rental, 'or upon any other Terms that may be Deemed reasonable'.[32]

The reason given for not completing to New Hall was that the ground leaked—though Colmore said this ceased within a year—and although it was through the same ground that the Farmer's Bridge locks were later to be built. Brindley, however, told the committee he felt Brickkiln Piece to be by far the best site for a terminus and the Assembly agreed.

Colmore therefore sought a mandamus from King's Bench. The General Assembly opposed, fortified by counsel's opinion that they were merely empowered to continue to New Hall, but not compelled. The motion for a mandamus was laid aside on 25 May and discharged on 28 September. In November, therefore, Colmore petitioned the House of Commons for leave to bring in a Bill to compel completion to New Hall, saying he would not have supported the original Act had he known the terminus would be elsewhere; permission was granted on 6 December. A special Assembly was called, at which a motion that an attempt be made to reach an accommodation was defeated by 114 votes to 210, and the committee were given powers to fight the Bill. In spite of all their efforts, however, which included a petition from some of Colmore's tenants who said the proposed extension would reduce the value of their property, the Bill became law at the end of February 1771.[33] It ordered the company to complete the canal by 25 March 1772, 'in as straight and direct a line as the level will admit'.

It might seem that the matter was now settled, but that was to reckon without Samuel Garbett who now reappeared as Colmore's agent. The main problem was the price of the land for the canal, or even its availability, since the two of them were determined, if possible, to prevent completion to Brickkiln Piece. On their part the company were determined to do, and to give, no more than they were compelled. They refused, for example, to cut the canal wider than normal to allow for the erection of wharves; on his part Colmore refused to let them cross his land to enter Brickkiln Piece. Even for the land needed towards New Hall he asked £32 per acre annual rent, 'An extraordinary price', as Dr Ash put it, 'to pay for Land whence we are compelled to go; and,' he added, 'not to be submitted to'.[34] The committee decided to apply for commissioners to decide the price, but Colmore then offered his land once again at £4 per acre 'if they were engaged to accommodate the *Publick* by making a sufficient Bason for Boats either near Friday Street or at any other Point ... in the Course ... to New Hall'.[35] After some bickering about what was meant by 'a sufficient Bason' the offer was rejected, the jury met on 18 August and awarded Colmore, on compulsory rental, £4.50 per acre for the land already cut and that needed to complete to Brickkiln Piece (nearly three acres) and £21.50 per acre for that needed to complete to New Hall (just over one acre). A few skirmishes remained but Brindley was able to report the canal complete and navigable by 25 March 1772.

At the other end there had also been trouble, though of a different kind. In January 1770 the committee of the Staffs & Worcs Canal ordered that their clerk 'do to Morrow write to the Proprietors of the Birmingham Navigation ... to be informed by what time they will compleat their Cut to make a Communication'.[36] The reply was slow in coming, though the Birmingham Canal were taking some steps beyond Oldbury, and thinking of more. The trouble was that the exact route was still undecided—and when it was finally planned it was so circuitous as to lead to the suggestion that Samuel Simcock had used it as a means of immortalising his initials!

At the Wolverhampton end Brindley at first suggested that there was too little water for 6ft locks, and suggested that they should be 3ft deep and the extreme lock 6ft. Apart from the fact that this would have necessitated forty locks, it ignores the fact that the loss of water is regulated by the largest lock. The first fact was presumably realised before the flight was built, but not the second, since the last lock was still of double depth. By March

1770 work was sufficiently advanced for Brindley to be ordered 'that the extream Lock be set about' when the water was let out of the summit of the Staffs & Worcs Canal,[37] but money was none too plentiful (the ninth call of 10 per cent was made at this time, with much still to be done) and the pace was too slow for the other canal. They waited upon the Birmingham Canal committee to inform them of their resolution 'immediately to set about to make sure [we] compleat the Navigation' unless assurances were given that the Birmingham Canal would do so 'with all convenient and reasonable Expedition'.[38] However, the General Assembly of the Birmingham Canal, though it agreed to build a new Navigation Office, two houses for clerks and an adjoining coffee-house or tavern and to pay interest on calls to 31 March, did not, apparently, consider this matter.

After some months' more delay the Staffs & Worcs Canal decided to take counsel's opinion, since the lack of connection with the coal-fields meant loss of revenue. A renewed approach was apparently made to the Birmingham Canal, for in August Brindley was called to the committee to see what orders he had given for completion. He reported progress which, he said, 'appeared to me Satisfactory', but the General Assembly in September felt that 'there appear'd a great deal of money expended for the quantity of work done since the first of September 1769', and set up a sub-committee to investigate.[39] There appeared to be some complaint about Beswick, the contractor, who was not finishing the work as he should, though this seems to have been settled satisfactorily, since, upon the conclusion of his contract, he was given another.

In December, seven months after the canal should have been completed, the Staffs & Worcs Canal inserted a statement in the press alleging that work was proceeding too slowly. The Birmingham committee inserted a reply, but words were not enough. On 31 January 1771 a petition was presented to the House of Commons in the name of the Staffs & Worcs company for leave to bring in a Bill to compel completion since, as a result of the delay, the price of Coals is reduced near One Half at the said Town of Birmingham, and is greatly advanced in other Parts ... and thereby that is made a private and local Advantage to the said town of Birmingham only, which was originally intended as a public Benefit—[40]

a claim which contrasts strangely with those being made at the same time in the petitions for completion at the other end!

The Birmingham Canal counter-petitioned, but being rather beset in the Parliamentary field at the time, tried arbitration. On 23 February the Earl of Dartmouth was agreed as umpire and within a week a settlement was reached, usually known as the 'Deed of Compromise'. This is nowhere recorded in minutes, but its outline is clear from an (undated) letter to Dartmouth from Sir Edward Lyttleton:

> It was unanimously agreed by the whole of each Party, that the Calls should be made as high and as fast as possible, & that 7 tenths, as well of the Calls as of the Tonnage, should be paid for the Completion of the Birmingham Canal to Autherley, & that no Money should be expended in Building Warehouses Etc., till the Junction of the two Canals was made,

the Birmingham Company to pay the expenses of the application to Parliament and to have use of such of the money set aside as was surplus to requirements, 'on their giving Security for the Repayment of it when wanted'.[41] On 14 April the Commons were informed that the committee to which the petitions had been referred 'was dropped' and a proposal to revive it was lost by 26 votes to 94.

Once a settlement was reached, action was prompt. Trustees were set up and the treasurer ordered to pay in the necessary money; as many planks and barrows as could be spared were sent to Wolverhampton, 'there to be repair'd and used in the course of the Canal beyond Bilston', and Mr Tomkyss was told the committee insisted he fulfil his contract for 2 million bricks.[42] As a result, by August 1771 the canal was open to Wolverhampton, but money was again short. Counsel's opinion was sought and he

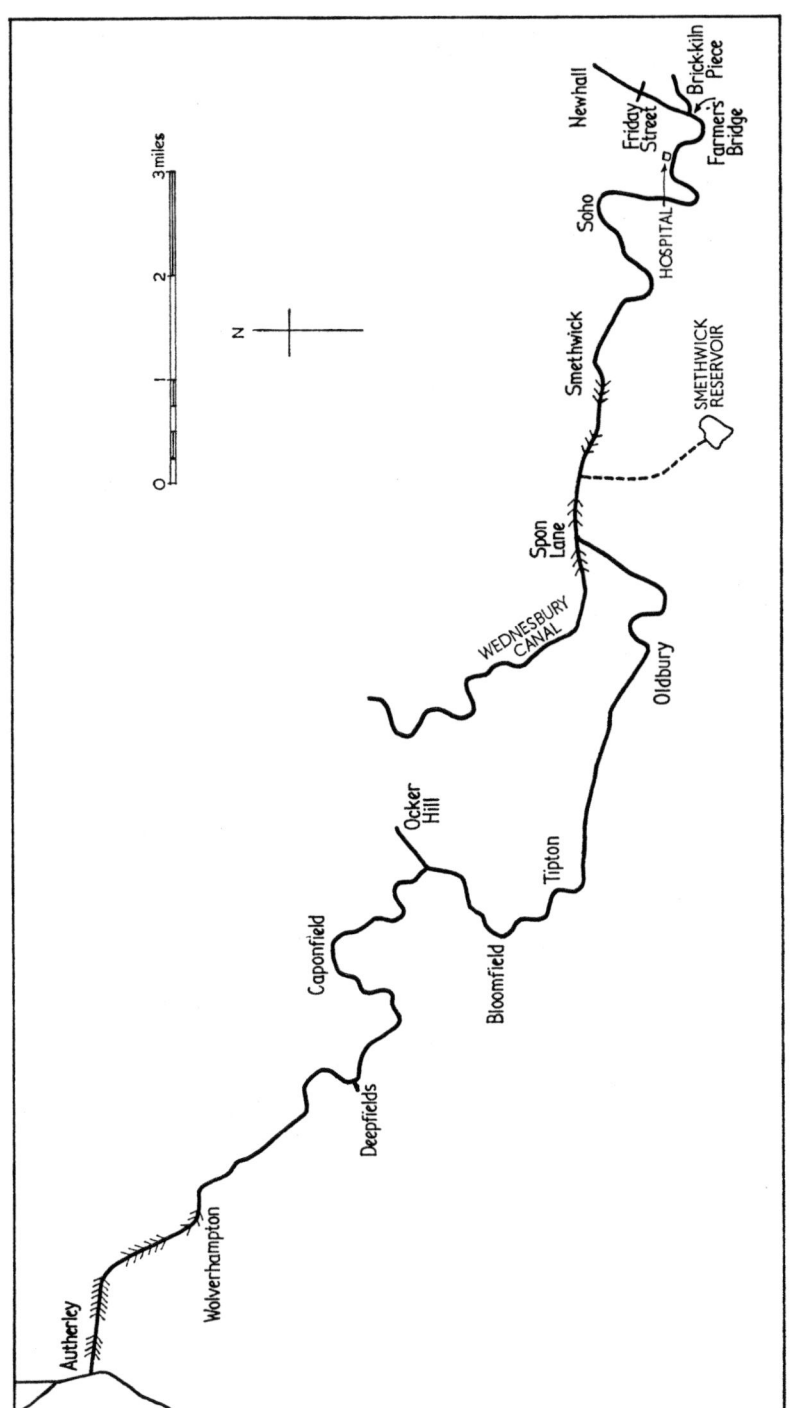

FIGURE 1 Map of the first canal, 1772

advised that it might be difficult to borrow on the security of the tolls as that was not specifically authorised in the Act. It was therefore decided to raise a further £20,000 by calls.

The rush to finish the work did not make for efficiency. In May 1772 Brindley reported

> that the Iron Work & also the Wood work of the Locks at W Hampton under the deed of Compromise were very badly executed, particularly that the wood work was ill tenanted & Mortized & the Iron work bad teeth & pinions & that it is absolutely necessary the same should be altered[43]

At the same time water was turned into the Wolverhampton summit, much of it coming from mines pumping engines, and it was agreed to build four cottages for lock-keepers, near the first, fifth, tenth and fifteenth locks, with a reservoir between the seventeenth and nineteenth 'for supplying the Large Lock at the Junction at Autherley'.[44] Milestones had been set up from Brickkiln Piece to Autherley and a collateral branch begun at Ocker Hill.

In August the two companies agreed to share the expense of a bridge at the junction, and that the connection be opened before 14 September. The committee demurred, since the towing path and bridges were reported incomplete, but it was finally opened on 21 September.

Thus the canal as originally planned was at last complete, just over four and a half years after cutting began. On 27 September the General Assembly resolved 'that Mr. Brindley be settled with and paid in full as the Company's Engineer up to the 29th day of September Instant . . . Nevertheless that they shall always be desirous of his Advice upon the Companys affairs when they may require the Assistance of an Engineer.'[45]

Brindley died the same day.

CHAPTER 2

Rivalries and Expansion, 1772–85

THE DUDLEY CANAL AND TUNNEL

THE success of the Birmingham Canal encouraged imitation. In February 1775 a 'numerous meeting', attended by Meredith on behalf of the Birmingham company, adopted a plan for a canal from Stourton to the collieries near Stourbridge. The Birmingham committee were aware that this might represent a threat to them via the interests of their customers and took part in a meeting with the proposers of the new canal and the Staffs & Worcs Canal, whose revenues were threatened. A survey was ordered of water sources and of pit-head prices of coal, to see whether tonnage rates would have to be reduced.

On the other side, 'Your Friend' told the readers of *Aris's Birmingham Gazette*:

> Their Opposition would . . . appear to be SELFISH and MERCENARY . . . why should the Trade and Prosperity of a populous and manufacturing County suffer for the sake of enriching a Company of Proprietors whose Profits are well known to be double of what they ought to be,

and argued that if Bilston coal were replaced at Stourport, it would become cheaper in Birmingham. The committee privately felt they were on weak ground in opposing this 'general View of public Utility, that was the Ostensible motive at least for our own Undertaking' but felt 'an Opposition may be supported on ye ground, of depriving the Coal Owners . . . near Bilston of their accustomed Trade solely to give that Benefit to . . . almost a sole Proprietor [Lord Dudley] of Coal Mines in another County.'[1]

It was decided to petition against the Bill, now in the form of a canal from Stourton to Dudley. At first there was an alliance with the Staffs & Worcs Canal, but the latter managed 'to Obtain a private Satisfaction for their Company', and withdrew. The Bill failed to pass all its stages but was re-presented in the new Session as two Bills, the original Stourton–Stourbridge Canal first. In spite of renewed opposition they passed their crucial vote in June 1776 by 60–21 and made their first calls three months later.[2]

The Acts contained clauses protecting the water-supply of the Birmingham Canal, restraining the new canals from

> extending, at any Time, the Canal . . . or the Collateral Cuts . . . to any Place or Places whatsoever, lying or being within the Distance of One Mile and a Half [Dudley Canal : One Mile] of the Birmingham Canal Navigation . . . either by Canal, Cut, Sluice, Tunnel, or otherwise howsoever,

and from taking water that could supply the Birmingham Canal.

The two canals thus began in closely connected fashion and, at first, were linked in committees and personnel, including sharing their clerk and engineer. As late as 1801, in fact, the Dudley Canal appointed James Green, engineer of the Stourbridge Canal, to the same post with them, each canal paying him £35pa. In 1788 a plan for amalgamation was seriously discussed but dropped when the Selly Oak extension was begun. However, in spite of this, their destinies diverged thereafter, probably because of the differing needs of their areas; the Dudley Canal served coal-producers, the Stourbridge Canal the coal-using glass works who were always influential in its councils. The Stourbridge Canal never became part of the BCN and retained its independent existence until nationalisation.

The first general meeting of the Dudley Canal was held in June 1776, elected a committee and appointed Thomas Dadford, senior, as their surveyor at not more than £80pa. It was agreed that boats passing a lock should be charged 6d (2½p) a ton, with a reduction to 2d for lime and limestone.

The line had been laid down in the Act only in general terms. Dadford was asked to survey two alternative routes, one with and one without locks, and it was decided to adopt that which ran from two termini at Netherton—at Great and Little Ox Leasow—and running to Dudley Wood without a lock. For some reason the Little Ox Leasow termination was later abandoned, Thomas Foley, the landowner and the other main promoter of the canal, being given £100 compensation, 'towards Establishing a New Colliery by the side of the said Canal'.[3] Lord Dudley was given £700 compensation because the canal kept thus entirely to the upper level. (It should be noted that the total length of the canal was only 2¼ miles and the capital £7,000.)

Dadford contracted with John Beswick for the cutting, with John Brown 'to compleat and finish the Stone Work and Tunnell of our Lock' and with George Making for 'the Hollow Coyns in our Lock . . . as also to pare and joint the Gates in the Stone Work belonging to the said Lock'[4]—which is confusing, to say the least, for there were nine locks at Black Delph and the junction was at the bottom. Each contractor was paid as he completed each section of his work.

Construction of the locks began in July 1777, with a fall of 10ft each, but as construction continued money became scarce. By mid-1778 all the £7,000 authorised had been called up (though only £6,600 had been received since the company had £400 of forfeited shares) and the canal was still not complete. It was therefore decided to continue calls until another £1,000 had been raised. By the end of 1778, another £23 per share had been called and money was still needed; another £1,000 was therefore raised, part of which came from loans.

By this time, however, the main construction work was nearly complete; a wharf and lockhouse were planned and a feeder laid out across the Dudley–Netherton turnpike via Little Ox Leasow, Cinder Banks and Baptist End—not, apparently to a reservoir, for the first mention of such was of an agreement with the Stourbridge Canal in mid-1779 to build one south-east of the turnpike and below the Dudley summit, to raise water by an engine.

It was also decided to build a reservoir of their own on Pensnett Chase between the canal and the Dudley–Brierley Hill–Brettell Lane turnpike, with a dam 25ft high and a feeder leading into the existing feeder, which presumably tapped surface drainage. Although it was still felt that new sources of water were necessary, it was agreed that, as the Stourbridge Canal had paid £75 towards the cost of the feeder, they could have water from the reservoir when water flowed over the uppermost lock weir, 'Such Weir to be always kept one Inch and an half lower than the flood weirs'.[5] This, however, was after the canal was open and used. The actual date is not given in the minutes, but it is clear that it was open in the latter half of 1779, before the Stourbridge Canal, though it could have carried little traffic until the latter opened on 3 December.

In March 1783 the company became apprehensive about a clause in the Birmingham Canal Bill of that year which would have empowered that company to make partial reductions of tonnage, since they feared this would enable them to reduce the price of Bilston coals at Stourport. The clause was withdrawn, but could be revived, and it was probably from this danger that the solution emerged of a junction with the Birmingham Canal, first mooted at a meeting between the two canals 'at Lord Dudley's' in December 1783.

In January 1785 a joint committee was set up of the Dudley and Stourbridge Canals to petition for a Bill to effect the junction and to negotiate with the Birmingham Canal about compensation tolls. It was proposed to use Lord Dudley's Canal and Tunnel at Tipton which had been the cause of much trouble to the Birmingham Canal some years previously, when they had discovered that Lord Dudley was attempting, without permission, to effect a communication with his Tipton colliery (via an open canal) and the Castle Mill lime workings (by a tunnel). He had stubbornly defended his 'right' to cut as he pleased and considerable argument took place before agreement was reached and the cut made. This was (and is, since not all of it was utilised in the new canal) known as Lord Ward's Canal, and the intention was to build a tunnel from the lime-works basin to the Dudley Canal at Park Head.

It was argued that more Bilston coal would be sold and that the Birmingham Canal would save the water and the expense of repairing the locks at Autherley! It was planned to build four new reservoirs and to pump from Busseys Hollows, beside the water 'expected to arise in the Tunnel'. In order to avoid disputes as to the taking of water from each other's summits, a double stop-gate was suggested in Lord Dudley's Canal, 'which would neither give or take more water at any one time than the quantity contain'd in the Lock of the difference of the height of the respective Summits at the same time'.[6] The Birmingham company asked Smeaton for advice, with what result is not recorded.

The Staffs & Worcs Canal, not surprisingly, decided to oppose, as did the Oxford and Coventry Canals, who foresaw nothing but loss from a new outlet for Black Country coals. The Birmingham Canal, however, could be bought off and, therefore, while using the others, were unwilling to commit themselves in a way which would prevent a profitable outcome.

The main problems were loss of tonnage revenue and loss of water. On the latter, James Watt, who at this period served the company in an advisory capacity as surveyor on several occasions, advised that, for full safety, the Dudley Canal should lock down 4ft, 'but that, it was necessary for perfect security that the Dudley Canal should be at least two feet higher in Level'. The Dudley Canal expressed themselves willing to agree, though it is hard to see how it could be possible if Lord Ward's Canal were to be used. In the end, it was agreed to use 'a Lock with double Setts of Gates' with the Dudley Canal at least 6in higher.[7] John Snape, the engineer, was closely questioned about water in the Parliamentary committee and gave his sources as rivulets, which 'may run to Mills but . . . do not fall into the Stour or into the Birmingham Canal', and mines water. (He was also questioned on his experience of tunnelling, which he said was none, and as to his examination of strata, which he said was 'impossible, without boring Holes at every few Yards'!)[8]

C

On the question of tonnage, it was agreed that the Birmingham Canal should be given 9d per ton on all coal and ironstone passing out of that canal above the first lock at Riders Green or raised within one mile of the canal, with 1s 1d (5½p) per ton if passing one or more locks below Riders Green; for all other merchandise the rate should be 1s 5½d (7½p), in all cases exclusive of the normal tonnage on the canal. Nevertheless the Birmingham company petitioned against the Bill, presumably as a means of keeping up the pressure.

Meanwhile, controversy continued in the press. An anonymous Birmingham native, now resident in London, spoke of the town as preparing to throw away 'that invaluable Blessing which Nature has bestowed on you . . . COAL', since it would be exhausted by sales to distant markets, but he was assured, by one who was 'well informed, that my Lord Dudley . . . alone . . . has coal sufficient to supply the Markets for upwards of one Thousand Years'.[9]

But this was merely the froth; the main matter had been settled when the Birmingham Canal was bought off. The Act received the Royal Assent on 4 July 1785.[10] Besides the agreed tolls it made it incumbent upon the Dudley Canal to erect a stop-lock

> furnished with Three or Four Gates or Four Pair of Gates, Two of which Gates, or Pairs of Gates, shall be placed at such Distance as to admit the Boats . . . into the Body of the Lock between the said Gates, in the same Manner as in any common Lock; and the said Two Gates . . . shall be made to open in such Direction as to maintain the Waters of the said intended Canal on a higher level than the Waters of the said [BCN] . . . and the said Gate, or Third and Fourth Pair of Gates shall be situated within or without the Body or Chest of the Lock . . . at some convenient . . . Distances from the lower or upper . . . Pair of Gates last mentioned and shall be so constructed as to prevent the water . . . from running into the said intended Canal.

Perhaps not surprisingly, the construction of this lock was to prove a major bone of contention.

The shares were increased by another 200, only 45 of which

were taken up by the old shareholders, the remainder being sold to 67 members of the public; the accounts for the new section were kept separate from the old. An advertisement and specification were issued for the tunnel,

> to be executed by the Yard forwards, including the sinking of the Shafts, driving the Headway, widening the same to contain the Brickwork . . . to be made nine feet three Inches wide, five feet six Inches deep in Water, and seven feet high above Top Water, and to be continued from End to End in a straight Line; the Centers to be made three Inches higher than the above Dimension to allow for sinking of the Arch, the bottom to be an inverted Arch of Culver Bricks of four and a half Inches, on sound Foundation, and nine Inches on spongy hands . . . the Side Walls and Top Arch to be nine Inches thick, and where it shall be found necessary, the Side Walls to be fourteen Inches thick, the Top of the Arch to be clayed four Inches thick, and Brick Ends or other sound Materials laid thereon, so as to conduct the Water in small Streams down the Outside of the Brick Work, thence through small Inlets into the Tunnel.[11]

The successful contractor was John Pinkerton, and his contract was endorsed three months later, with William Jessop as his security for £4,000.[12]

Dadford reported that five locks were necessary and John Wildgoose was appointed surveyor at £60pa to assist him. A few months later trouble began with Pinkerton, Wildgoose being told to 'pay strict Attention to the execution of the Tunnel by Mr. Pinkerton . . . and particularly that they do not suffer any soft or bad bricks to be made use of', upon pain of dismissal for neglect. Less than a fortnight later a special meeting had to be called to authorise the treasurer to pay Pinkerton £500 on account above his agreed weekly payments (£150) and he was ordered to pay, in future, 'Such Sum of Money only, as Abraham Lees & John Wildgoose shall certify to be actually expended in the Course of such Week'. The next year all orders empowering the treasurer to pay money to Pinkerton were rescinded, Richard Aston was ordered to set out the cutting for the north entrance and Isaac Pratt for the south 'so as not in any way to interfere with any part of the Tunnel included in the contract with Mr. J^{no} Pinkerton', and Pinkerton and Jessop were ordered to attend the committee.[13]

A meeting between the committee's representatives and Pinkerton, accompanied by his attorney, took place at Lord Dudley's London house on 11 May 1787, at which the company refused to accept a suggestion that his contract be waived and the value of the work done left to arbitration. They also refused an offer of £1,500, asking £2,000, payable by instalments, with good security, 'as they have not the least Confidence in his personal Security alone', and claiming that even so they would lose upwards of £2,000 since 'many Applications made by Contractors [show] that the Tunnel may be compleated at the Price agreed'. Pinkerton claimed that his over-expenditure was 'on account of the extreme hardness of the strata, and the immense quantities of water it made, a circumstance not apprehended from the information which had been collected from the more intelligent colliers in the neighbour hood', but, under threat of legal proceedings, agreed to pay the £2,000.[14]

By this time the 'old' proprietors had paid £200 per share and each share was therefore divided into two. At the beginning of 1789 new shares had to be issued to raise another £5,000 for completion, new proprietors were told that there would be no interest and told that all income was to go for maintenance. Not surprisingly, some proprietors fell into arrears and legal action was threatened. Since the Old Canal was making profits above maintenance the surplus was lent, at interest, to the New Canal to complete the tunnel, which was progressing slowly and out of line. In 1790 a new Act[15] gave powers to raise another £10,000 in a hundred new shares amongst the existing proprietors and to borrow £5,000. By June 1792 contractors were being sought for arching 'that part of the Tunnel which remains unarched' and over a year later handbills were printed saying the tunnel was open and completely navigable, though it had been announced as open in the press ten months previously.

A sum of £42,754 had been spent and, after paying interest to

September 1792 and borrowing another £3,000, there was £1,191 to complete the necessary reservoirs. At this stage the two groups of shareholders were amalgamated, resulting in a total of 513¼ shares, with a capital of £59,325. To celebrate, a new seal was adopted, with the company's name, the tunnel entrance, pit-head gear and a beam engine.

There remained the problem of the stop-lock. The first model having been found to differ from the one described in the Act of Parliament was rejected by the Birmingham company in August 1791 and it was another year before agreement was reached, the stop-lock being sited inside the tunnel and opened in mid-1793. The site was apparently not satisfactory; the Dudley committee suggested a new one on 'the South side of the Bridge at the Tipton pieces' and the Birmingham committee, on one of their tours of inspection, agreed that it was 'in a very inconvenient situation—the House provided by that Co for this Company's Agent near half a Mile distant from the Lock & the Road to & fro' very dangerous especially in Wett or Frosty Weather when the overhanging Rocks shiver & fall upon the Path'.[16] For some reason they did not learn of the Dudley company's agreement until a year later but the go-ahead was given soon afterwards, involving a new cut joining the Birmingham Canal nearer to Tipton.

This did not end disagreement. In December 1797 the Dudley lock-keeper replaced the bolt by one considered insufficient, as a result of which the BCN affixed a padlock, which was taken off. The outcome is not recorded. Perhaps more important, by the end of the century the Dudley company began to realise that they were losing by their agreement since, it was alleged, the Birmingham company were raising their weirs—and the water had to be kept 6in above them on the Dudley side. As a result, if the agreement were operated 'there would not be sufficient height in the Dudley Tunnel for the passage of several sorts of Merchandise'. They therefore kept the level low and passage was refused through the lock. The BCN claimed that the weirs had been raised, but just before the Act; the Dudley committee received information, '& particularly from Joseph Allen this [Birmingham] Companys Tenant on the spot,' that the weirs had been raised just after the Act, and renewed their pressure, counsel's opinion being sought. As the Birmingham Canal 'declined an amicable adjustment' legal steps were taken but with what result is not known.[17]

THE FAZELEY ROUTE

Meanwhile the Birmingham Canal had begun to expand to the east of the ridge. The first suggestion for this had come as early as 1773 with a suggestion from the Oxford Canal for a link at first to near Coventry, later to Fazeley but, after some discussion and surveying, it was decided a line to Napton would be 40 miles shorter and an abortive subscription was opened for that route.

The next mention of a canal to Fazeley was as a rival, not an extension; in August 1781 the Oxford Canal Assembly agreed to proceed with a canal from 'Bilston, Sedgeley and Wednesbury' to Fazeley, with a branch to Deritend. An anonymous writer immediately suggested to the public that, as the Birmingham Canal would 'probably very soon' be extended to the mines on the Lower Level near Wednesbury and Bilston,

> the Purposes of the Public would be much better answered by a Canal, from the Birmingham Canal ... to Napton, which would go through a Country chiefly supplied with Coal from Birmingham by Land ... Whereas the Scheme ... seems calculated only to answer partial and private Purposes[18]

The anonymous author must have been privy to the innermost thoughts of the Birmingham committee, for the extension to the lower level is not mentioned in the minutes until December, when it was decided to survey a route and, almost immediately, to apply for an Act. Next month the petition for the Bill for the Fazeley Canal was presented, and battle was joined.

The main basis for the Birmingham Canal's case was their 'interest'. As Samuel Galton put it:

> Is it prudent in the Public to discourage Adventurers in canal making who not withstanding all their hazard gain but little ...

and don't it seem Unjust in the Public not only to deprive those who happen to be fortunate of that little to make them Losers... certain it is that if the Public adopt the Principle of disregarding how far the New Canals may Interfere with Old Ones most of the Old Companys if not Every One may be Ruined,

and the company claimed that their Shares had been 'bought upon the Faith of Parliamentary Security, and which to many Widows, Orphans and others is their only support'.[19]

Permission to bring in the Fazeley Bill was granted on 1 March; on 19 March it, and the Birmingham Canal Extension Bill, were defeated, the vote on the latter being 47-45.

The first round was thus over, but both parties realised it was not the end. The Birmingham Canal called a special Assembly to recommend the building of a 'continuation of the Canal to Digbeth'—an extension from New Hall down and round the north and east of the town so as to make any approach from Fazeley by a rival canal impossible—in spite of warnings that this was unlawful as being a branch of more than one thousand yards in length. Application to Parliament was renewed for the extension to the Lower Level and a plan was ordered of a canal from Fazeley, via 'Walsall, Catshill etc.' to 'such lower level'.

The petition for the rival canal was presented on 6 December, and letters were sent out to organise counter-petitions. When there nevertheless appeared 'great reason to apprehend that Powers will be granted ... in a manner which may be extremely injurious', to the Birmingham company it was decided to petition for powers to build it themselves, and a Bill to this effect was brought in at the end of January.[20]

'Both parties beat up for volunteers in the town, to strengthen their forces; from words of acrimony, they came to those of virulence, then the powerful batteries of hand-bills and newspaper were opened',[21] the Birmingham company making great play with the allegation that 150 of their shares belonged to widows and orphans and that 'the profits of the new-intended Canal are to arise from a deduction in the profits of the present Canal'.[22] They were aware that their opponents had agreed with the Coventry,

Oxford and Trent & Mersey canal companies at Coleshill the previous summer to work together to complete the first two and agreed to accept the same obligation. Their opponents asked of their proposed line:

> Is it to serve the Coal Owners?—No—they *petition against it*—Is it because there is not Coal sufficient . . . on the Banks of the present Canal?—No—*the Owners of the Coal cannot send it to market for want of water in the present Canal*—Is it for want of sufficient Trade to pay them a proper Interest . . . ?—No, No—they divide immense profits, and sell their Shares TWO HUNDRED AND EIGHTY POUNDS PREMIUM . . . It is solely . . . *to monopolise all the Coal in many thousand acres of Mines.*[23]

> Are not the basest innovations made,
> That ever did a company degrade?
> Year after year, have they not filched away
> That from the town that would a levy pay!
> Yet fondly boast what Parliament has done,
> Cry up their faith, but never keep their own[24]

However, influence was more powerful than invective. A subcommittee of the Birmingham Canal sat continuously in London; they visited MPs and Lords, arranged and edited petitions, and agreed clauses to protect water. The new company's Bill was read a second time on 3 February and it was agreed to hear counsel on 6 February. This was deferred eight times until the Bill was shelved on 13 May, though the main debate was really on 31 January, when it was agreed to defer this Bill so that the two could be considered together. A belated attempt was made to defer the Birmingham company's Bill for consideration of a scheme to improve the Trent, Tame and Anker, at an alleged cost one-third that of the canal, but it was unsuccessful. At the third reading, 'when both parties had marshalled their forces, there was the fullest House of Commons ever remembered on a private Bill' and it became law at the end of June.[25]

The Act[26] was not only for the Fazeley line, but also for the extension to the lower level at Broadwaters with six collateral cuts including Toll End and Gospel Oak. It set up a new company with virtually the same proprietors as the old, to be known as the Birmingham & Fazeley Canal Navigation, with powers to raise £85,000 in 500 shares and £30,000 on mortgage. In the event the shareholders in the new company, excepting only the two new ones, handed over their powers to the old company, which by a new Act became 'the Company of the Birmingham and Birmingham and Fazeley Canal Navigations'.[27] The canal had to be completed by 24 June 1787 and begun at the same time at both ends (Sect VI) with at least £20,000 spent annually (Sect VII). Tonnage was fixed at 4d for going through a lock into the Birmingham Canal, 1½d per ton/mile if not entering the Coventry Canal, 10d per ton if so doing and ¾d per ton lock dues at Farmer's Bridge (Sect LXV). An extra 1d per ton was to be levied on all goods passing through the first Farmer's Bridge lock to pay the expenses of the subscribers to the rival canal, not to exceed £3,600 plus interest (Sect CXII). This latter was a deterrent to trade and the Birmingham Canal tried to pay it off by a lump sum, which was refused. At one stage they refused to pay over the money collected until they had been given the expenses of collection, but these were eventually fixed at 15 per cent annually and payments continued until the debt was extinguished early in the new century.

The Act also laid upon the Birmingham Canal the obligations accepted by its rival at Coleshill and this caused trouble immediately. Early in 1784 another meeting took place at Coleshill of the four companies concerned and it was agreed that all should start 'to execute their works at the point of Communication at Fazeley and lay out therein the Sum of One Thousand Pounds each',[28] the Birmingham Canal taking the stretch from Fazeley to Whittington Brook, the Trent & Mersey from thence to Fradley and the Coventry completing from Fazeley to Atherstone. After considerable argument, mainly over a proposed limitation of tonnage to 1d a mile to allow competition with Staffordshire coal and because the Birmingham Canal wished to insist on completion of the whole route to Oxford before making junction at

Fazeley, in the course of which the proposed river improvement was revived, agreement was embodied in a new Act.[29]

Meanwhile work had begun. In August 1783 the Birmingham Canal set out the line from New Hall and accepted a contract from John Pinkerton for the Broadwaters extension. He was again mentioned as 'engineer' for the Fazeley Canal in February 1784, at which date the Trent & Mersey also gave him the contract for the section from Fradley to Dennis Brook, it later being agreed he should continue to Fazeley for £8,716, including keeping the line in repair for three years. Thus quietly appeared on the scene the man who was to become the *bête noire* of the Birmingham Canal and to involve them in quarrels and litigation which outlasted the century.

By April 1784 he was so far advanced on the Broadwaters extension that he was complaining about a shortage of bricks 'so that he cannot connect this Work so as to finish and fill that part of the Canal with Water and thereby secure the Banks', but within six months it was resolved, as on the Dudley Canal, that no money be paid to him on account until he had 'measured up His work as far as He hath at present proceeded and delivered in a Bill of the same'.[30]

Tenders were requested for the line from Birmingham to Digbeth in November 1785, Pinkerton's arriving late. The section from Farmer's Bridge to Aston Junction was given to Thomas Sheasby, later an engineer in his own right on the South Wales canals; six months later he was also awarded the section from Digbeth to Minworth, Pinkerton being awarded the stretch from Minworth to Fazeley, all to be completed by midsummer 1787.

The Broadwaters extension was opened to Riders Green in October 1785, but it was reported 'left very incompleat' with 'Repairs reported to be wanting' so Pinkerton was told his account would not be settled until it was put right.[31] A report was also made by Bough and Beswick on the Fradley–Fazeley section and a copy sent to the Trent & Mersey company because 'the defects complained of are so various, and of such magnitude as seem to call for the serious attention of both Committees, that the Undertakers may forthwith amend the imperfections of their past Works and avoid similar errors in their future proceedings'. A deputation from the committee met the agent and engineer of the Trent & Mersey and went over the section:

> They found . . . that the part under execution by Mr. Pinkerton was very incompleat injudiciously laid out and in many places very defectively executed . . . particularly in the direction of the Canal which . . . is curved in a very improper manner the pudling benching and many other particulars . . . seem to have met with equal inattention . . . and in the General the defects are so notorious as not to require the Eye of an Engineer to discover them.[32]

There were further complaints the next year, but apparently they were settled, since final accounts were presented in July 1788, though Pinkerton did not announce the length as open until December.

As far as the Fazeley line was concerned he was operating without a contract, and one was not prepared until the beginning of 1787. A covenant was added both here and, in similar terms, in Sheasby's contract

> because of the circumstances in which Mr. Pinkerton then stood with the Dudley Company . . . enabling the Committee in case Mr. Pinkerton should neglect to proceed in the execution agreeable to their expectations to take the Works into their Hands and get the same executed . . . and to charge the expence thereof to Mr. Pinkertons Account'.[33]

Though dated 25 July 1786, the contract was not executed until 18 May 1787, committing Pinkerton to complete by 24 June 1788 for a price of £11,563, to be paid as work progressed, with £500 retained for three years, during which period he would keep the work in repair.

Meanwhile he had been held up because land had not been purchased which he required in order to make bricks and at the end of 1786 he reported that the levels were apparently wrong between Fazeley and Minworth. A re-survey by Bough and Pinkerton's nephew showed them to be out by 4ft 8in, and possibly more between Minworth and Birmingham. A re-survey by Bull confirmed this; the difference in cost was £1,400, which had lost Sheasby the contract, since Pinkerton had estimated on the basis of his own, correct, levels. The nephew felt that this, and other similar matters 'occasioned Mr. Bough to become a great enemy to Mr. Pinkerton'.[34]

The committee felt progress was slow and ordered a weekly report, with a check by Bough, who would not seem to have been the best person. Pinkerton admitted that 'the line [had] not the appearance ... of being pushed on with that resolution that you may think necessary', but claimed that it was essential to complete Fradley–Fazeley first in order to 'take the water after us till we get amongst the locks'.[35]

Sheasby was also under criticism for using bricks of 'totally unsuitable' quality but his locks at Farmer's Bridge were ready to be filled with water by November 1787, though the lock pounds were found leaky. Further complaints against both him and Pinkerton continued as the months passed, but those against Pinkerton were eventually given in greater detail when the case reached the courts. It was alleged that, instead of puddling, gutters were filled with 'soil, gravel or sand', 'that such bad bricks were used they could scarce find enough for fronts', 'that bricks were laid without mortar and mortar without bricks', and much more in the same strain.[36] More seriously, it was alleged that 'there was such constant failures in the embankments, bridges, locks &c, that it could never be clearly ascertained when the canal was completed'. Many locks had to be taken down and rebuilt; 'when a boat went in and out [of the fifth lock] the whole face and back of the walls would move'.[37]

Whatever the workmanship, in late 1788 he began to exceed his estimates and money was cut off, pending 'a particular Acct of the nature of His Extra Works, as well that already done as that remaining to be finished'. At the same time Shaw, the superintendent of works, was sacked for his 'connivance at the late transactions in the Works under your immediate inspection'.[38] Notwithstanding this, Pinkerton claimed the canal would be complete in six months, but he was removed from the works in

February 1789. The first commercial boat passed along on 11 August, the committee having travelled over the line in their boat six days previously, viewing 'the Ruins of the Coventry Com^{ys} Aqueduct at the River Tame' which rendered the completion useless for southbound traffic for a twelve month. In December, however, the navigation was stopped by the failure of two of the Curdworth locks; this was the beginning of a long saga, not to end until thirty-five years later, when a report on repairs could finally state:

> As respects the Locks at Curdworth & Dunton which were built by the renowned Mr. Pinkerton & which have in truth proved so costly to the Company it is proper to remark that the work necessary to put them in a tollerable state of security may now be considered as done.[39]

The financial problem was rather less long-lasting, but equally troublesome. It revolved round the precise amounts owed by Pinkerton to the company for over-expenditure and in the other direction for necessary extra work and rising costs. The case dragged on until 1801, with Pinkerton using every possible delay and producing new accounts at intervals, until the matter was finally settled at arbitration, the company being ordered to pay Pinkerton £436 in full settlement, each side bearing their own costs. Pinkerton immediately published an account, in full, of the arbitration, including many personal attacks on Houghton as the chief of the 'miserable description of agents . . . who have occasioned all this mischief'. As a result Houghton brought an action, the book was found 'a scandalous and malicious Libel' and Pinkerton was fined £200 and imprisoned for a month. The General Assembly, resolving that this was 'highly proper', paid Houghton's costs and gave him £500.[40]

While not particularly savoury, the whole episode is most enlightening as to eighteenth-century contracting, especially the lack of adequate estimating, costing and supervision. It also throws a flood of light on the inadequacies of the men available for the technical posts at a time when demand was fast outrunning supply and training.

CHAPTER 3

New Canals, 1790–1830

CANALS TO WORCESTER AND WARWICK

THE canals in this section are important to our story only in so far as they affected the interests of other canals, since they never became part of the BCN.

There was no doubt that the route from Birmingham to Worcester, via Autherley, was most circuitous; moreover it utilised the Severn, which was liable to shoaling, and necessitated transhipment at Stourport. The first proposal for a new canal, however, merely proposed to by-pass the Severn, by a route from Worcester to Stourbridge, obviously opposed by the Staffs & Worcs Canal, though the Birmingham Canal, whose solicitor had been engaged by the subscribers, 'but merely as a professional Man', 'desire[d] to be excused taking any active part in the Matter'.[1] Not many opponents took such extreme measures as a barber of Stourport, 'an extraordinary instance of the depravity of human nature', who, finding himself shaving the solicitor to the proposed canal, 'shocking to relate . . . as soon as he had him in the suds, cut his throat!—The motive . . . is supposed to arise from his apprehension, that if the proposed canal should take place, he would not have a man to shave at Stourport',[2] but many must have shared his apprehensions. However, the project was thrown out by the House of Lords and when it was raised again it was in the form of a barge canal direct from Birmingham to Worcester, first made public at a meeting in Bromsgrove in January 1790.

The Birmingham company did not discuss the matter in committee as much as might have been expected, but decided to ask for a clause forbidding communication with their canal, and concentrated action on this while the Bill was on its way through Parliament. After a certain amount of manoeuvring a motion to throw out the Bill was carried 52–29 on 15 April 1790, the bells being rung in Wolverhampton when the news was received. The Bill was re-presented in the next Session, its supporters taking particular care to allay fears that it would cause a coal shortage, and received the Royal Assent on 10 June 1791.[3] Much of the Act was devoted to water supply, denying the company the use of streams, reservoirs or steam engines between Birmingham and Tardebigge. The Birmingham Canal was safeguarded by a bar at the junction 7ft wide, ostensibly to save water, and the Dudley Canal was guaranteed an income equal to the average of that gained between 25 September 1792 and the completion of the new canal—which was to be longer than most expected.

The first level section was opened at the end of October 1795 and in April 1797 barges loaded with 60 and 80 tons passed through the newly opened tunnel, but increasing financial difficulties led to renewed recourse to Parliament in 1799. The next year an attempt was made to get the bar removed but no inducement was offered but surplus water, an offer being made, but to no avail, to raise the banks for this purpose. The bar was to remain until the canal was belatedly complete to the Severn in 1815.

The route to Warwick and Napton was more directly the concern of the Birmingham Canal. As we have seen, it was first suggested as a way of shortening the route to Oxford and was raised again as part of the battle over the low level canal but it did not become an economic proposition because of heavy lockage until the opening of the Grand Junction Canal offered the possibility of a direct canal route from Birmingham to London.

In July 1792 a deputation waited upon the Birmingham committee from the subscribers to a canal 'to be made between the 2nd Lock on the Digbeth Canal and the Towns of Stratford &

Warwick'[4] to see if there would be enough water. A survey revealed water, but at a considerable expense and the committee asked a duty of 6d (2½p) per ton on all goods from or into the new canal, finally accepting a reduction to 3d for goods going no further than Farmer's Bridge.

Local interests, however, felt differently, and a Town's Meeting was called to oppose the canal because it would take coals out of Birmingham, since coals had already been raised in price by the Fazeley Canal. Supported by a petition from 'near Five Thousand inhabitants', it suggested an alternative route from Dudley via Selly Oak and Lapworth and the supporters of the new canal agreed to change their junction from Digbeth to King's Norton on the Worcester Canal, especially willingly since the latter, seeking trade, did not require compensation. This was a direct threat to the Birmingham Canal who 'induced the Warwick Company to separate from the Stratford and to carry their Canal in a different line from Warwick to Birmingham',[5] and it was authorised in 1793, the same year as the now truncated Stratford-upon-Avon Canal. The junction was now at Digbeth, the Birmingham Canal building a flight of six locks down from the top of Aston locks to meet a similar flight going up on the Warwick & Birmingham Canal.

Because of the opportunities offered by the Grand Junction Canal, the Birmingham Canal and its Warwick satellite promoted a Bill for a further canal to link Warwick with Braunston. The petition was presented in February 1794, with the same subscribers as to the Warwick & Birmingham, opposed by the Worcester and Stratford Canals but backed by the BCN, 'as the said extension if carried into effect must be highly beneficial both to this Town and the Birm^m Canal Company'.[6] The Act was obtained without too much trouble and the next move was to oppose a junction between the Stratford and Warwick Canals at Lapworth, a petition being presented against the Bill on the grounds that this would divert traffic from which the Birmingham Canal received compensating tolls. However, the opposition was unsuccessful though the Stratford Canal had to pay a stiff toll

Page 49 (*above*) The Navigation Office of the Birmingham Canal in Paradise Street, Birmingham, where committee meetings were held: built 1771, demolished 1928; (*below*) Gas Street basin (Brick-kiln Piece). The basin is to the left and the bar-lock in the right centre

Page 50 (*above*) Spon Lane top lock, in the shadow of the motorway. This and the two others in the flight are the oldest surviving locks on the BCN; (*below*) Farmer's Bridge, the toll-office and toll-clerk's house from the top lock. The site of Newhall Ring (now built over) is off the picture to the left

of 11d per ton on all traffic passing the junction, which must have restricted the trade.

After this construction proceeded relatively uneventfully, the two canals being opened at the end of December 1799 by a boatload of coals from the Staffordshire Collieries meeting a boat-load of limestone from Napton 'their arrival . . . announced by the firing of cannon and ringing of bells'. *Aris* commented that 'the opening of these canals will be a vast advantage to the trade of BIRMINGHAM and the Metropolis'.[7]

It was certainly to be a vast, and costless, advantage to the trade of the Birmingham Canal.

THE SELLY OAK EXTENSION

Once the Worcester & Birmingham Canal was under construction the possibility arose of a new coal route by-passing the Birmingham Canal altogether, if the new canal could be joined to the Dudley Canal. At first this could take coal to the Severn, but the building of the Stratford Canal and the junction at Lapworth would open markets to the south as well. This was the time of the canal mania, when the earliest canals having proved profitable beyond the dreams of their promoters, plans for new ones filled the newspapers, in Birmingham as elsewhere. The days of reckoning and short money were to come later.

Almost before the new scheme had passed beyond the status of a rumour the Birmingham company were ready with an alternative. On 31 July 1792, a meeting was held in the Birmingham Hotel 'for the purpose of considering a Canal from or near Birmingham to or near Netherton' and it was decided to ask the Dudley Canal to cooperate. Not surprisingly, they replied that 'the said intended Canal was in contemplation of this Company as an extension of the Dudley Canal prior to such [meeting]' and 'in case such intended Canal should be carried into execution by any other set of Proprietors [it] will be destructive to the Interests of this Company', and resolved to apply to Parliament themselves for a route to the Worcester & Birmingham Canal.[8]

D

They were immediately opposed by the Birmingham company, who put forward the Netherton junction route, even though warned, correctly, that it would require either 'great Lockage or a very Long Tunnel' and even though the Dudley Canal asked their assistance in construction in return for the same tonnage as received from Birmingham to the lower lock at Smethwick. In their turn the Dudley Canal met the sponsors of the Birmingham Hotel meeting and agreed to combine forces to raise the necessary money, estimated at £90,000.

The Birmingham company decided on a route from the Tipton level for their junction canal and began attacks on the other plan in the way that had proved so successful in the past, emphasising their 'interest' and the widows and orphans, who were now revealed to have bought shares at a premium so that their real return was only 3 per cent. A London committee was set up, with headquarters at No 8 Haymarket; its minutes give an illuminating picture, albeit from one side, of the forces at work to influence an eighteenth century Parliament on a private measure. There is no doubt that this was the greatest threat to date to the Birmingham company's virtual monopoly of the coal trade, and it was accordingly bitterly fought until the last. The main question argued publicly was that of coal prices, the Birmingham company posing as supporters of the inward trade, claiming that they had

> not in one Instance promoted any Plan for carrying Coals *from* Birmingham, for the Extensions they have made, have been forced upon them by *new Schemers*, with a view to participate in the Profits of the Birmingham Canal, without rendering any Service to the Public.[9]

The Bill was read the first time on 24 December 1792, and the second reading was fixed for 6 February, later deferred to 11 February. Petitions flowed in thick and fast, many arranged by the London committee; Sir Robert Lawley, who appeared to be wavering, was reminded that the Birmingham Canal, in his county of Warwick, was threatened by 'a mere speculative Scheme for a Navigation in another County', help was given to the Grand Junction Canal in return for support on this issue and a case made out for the Duke of Bridgewater to share the threat to established interests. Hastily jotted minutes and tasks to be done reveal the atmosphere: 'Mr. Perry Recommends Petitions . , . from Colne Brook Dale and the Barge Owners of the Severn —too late . . . Mr. T. Kelly Wine Merc^t—will call has a relation in Parl^t . . . what questions to be asked the opposition witnesses'. Cards were sent to 58 MP's in the names of the Duke of Bridgewater and the Marquess of Stafford requesting support. Unfortunately the Duke's name was used without authority and the cards had to be got back.[10] Nevertheless, the line-up of support and opposition was as might have been predicted, and the second reading was deferred again and again. In the meantime a petition had been presented for the Birmingham Canal's line to Netherton; it was referred to a committee but never reappeared, apparently because opposition was too strong. Presumably the other side were equally active, but less concerned to preserve a record; they were certainly more successful.

On the critical day of the second reading (20 February) the House refused, by 42–23, to hear counsel and sent the Bill to committee. On 23 February the London committee had a serious look at the position and set out certain questions to be resolved:

1st   In what way can the Netherton be opposed
2nd Whether it shall be opposed
3rd   If opposed, what Members shall be applied to . . .
4th   What Clauses shall be proposed to be added . . . or altered . . .
7th   Quere whether it be advisable to delay by any means the present Bill, for the purpose of gaining the assistance of the friends to the Warwick Bill when that Bill is passed.[11]

All was in vain; the Bill was reported on 18 March and an attempt to defeat it was lost, 20–48. Opposition continued in the Lords, the House being forced to sit for several hours on the subject on 1, 4, 9 and 14 May, but the Earl of Dartmouth was not the powerful politician he had been. All amendments were lost and the Act received the Royal Assent on 17 June.

Despite the long struggle the Act[12] was very little altered from the form in which it had been submitted. It permitted the raising of £90,000 in £100 shares with £40,000 more if necessary by shares or borrowing. No water could be taken from the Birmingham Canal (Sect X), 6d per ton was charged for entering the old canal from the extension, 3d per ton for entering from the Worcester & Birmingham Canal but not going through Lappal tunnel, and 2s (10p) per ton for traversing the tunnel (Sect XIV). The Worcester Canal, however, had to charge the same for goods between Selly Oak and King's Norton as between Birmingham and King's Norton and all goods for Birmingham were to be charged 2d a ton, irrespective of distance (Sect XXII). A stop-lock was to be erected at the junction similar to that at Tipton (Sects XXIII and XXVI). The dividends on the Stourbridge Canal were to be kept up to £12 per share by the Dudley Canal—provided the latter had already paid £5 on its own shares, which it did only once (Sects XXVII and XXVIII).

An anonymous correspondent, pointing out that coals by the new route into Birmingham would cost 2s 2d (11p) per ton as opposed to 1s 7½d (8p) by the old of which 1s 4½d (7p) went to the Birmingham Canal, added

> They have (I will not say how laudably) added by this *popular Act*, the modest trifle of 6d per ton . . . and I do not find that this additional charge is to be applied to any other than the laudable purpose of enriching a set of envious Speculators.[13]

This was sour grapes; could he have foreseen the difficulties to come he would not have envied the Dudley Canal their property.

Construction began immediately, William Clowes being appointed engineer at three guineas a day and William Underhill superintendent/surveyor at £150 annually, increased salaries which reflected the times. They were ordered to 'as much as possible avoid all deep cutting and embanking'. Cutting began at Selly Oak, Gosty Hill tunnel was begun in April 1794 and the clerk ordered to reside 'at or near Moor Street on the line of the Lappal Tunnel for the better Superintendence and Management of the Company's Concerns'. Work was proceeding apace on this tunnel, where dimensions were planned as 9ft 5in at top water tapering to a flat bottom 8ft 4in wide, with the water 5ft 6in deep and 7ft 6in headroom. A further problem was the aqueduct at Leasowes, Halesowen, which cut off a view, possibly designed by Capability Brown, and had therefore to be rendered ornamental.

Calls were made very fast as work progressed. £40 had been been called by October 1794 and £100 by July 1795; not surprisingly, by the end of 1794 there were £3,000 of arrears. Mineowners were called upon to open new mines along the route 'as being of the utmost importance to this Concern'.[14] The way this was pressed suggests that some at least of the new shareholders had bought more as speculators than as coalowners.

By this time engineering problems had arisen; the tunnel contractor had met hard rock, the level was wrong between Netherton and Halesowen and water was troublesome. Whitworth was called in to inspect the works and a sub-committee of four set up to supervise. Things were not helped by the financial crisis: 'The Treasurer is . . . in advance on the Company's Account . . . there is great defalcation in the payment of the Calls . . . the works cannot continue to be carried on unless some effectual Means are provided to raise Money'.[15] The treasurer agreed to lend £1,000 but this was a drop in the ocean; all the authorised £130,000 had been raised and spent and it was estimated £17,850 was still required. This sort of situation was, of course, not uncommon in 1796 and the Dudley Canal is remarkable more from the fact that it found means to overcome its difficulties than from their existence. Apparently most proprietors had been paying calls on the £40,000 of additional shares only, not on all shares. Therefore two calls were made, one of 10 per cent of £130,000 on those who had not thus paid and one of £4 8s 10½d (£4.44½) on those who had, a complicated method that became a feature of all future calls. In the meantime a new Act was obtained with little trouble authorising further calls, but financial trouble continued. A Special Assembly met in July 1797, by which time £25,000 had been called of the £40,000 allowed in the new Act, and the clerk was empowered to raise up to £13,528 to pay interest, complete the works and pay off £3,000 which had been borrowed on the security of individual members of the committee.

The clouds seemed to be lifting. The next regular Assembly heard the engineer report that the extension should be complete by Christmas and another attempt was made to get mines opened. The tunnel pumping engine and several horse-gins were sold and two ice-breakers bought, one for each end of the tunnel. By the new year *Aris* could announce 'with pleasure . . . that the Netherton Canal to Selly Oak is now finished, and will be navigable to Birmingham in a few weeks',[16] though, in fact, the junction was not yet cut. The line was opened by two boats which unloaded coal at the Worcester & Birmingham Canal's wharf in Birmingham in April 1798.

This was to be the last major change in the Dudley Canal while it remained independent. One or two minor straightenings were carried out, of which the biggest, a quarter-mile long cut-off at Lodge Farm, completed in 1838, involved a 75yd tunnel (later opened up) and a cost of £8,500, but even the collateral cuts provided for in the Act were not completed. That to Windmill End was carried out as far as it could go on the level and the colliery owners were then asked to connect to the basin at the end by tramroads, being allowed a reduction of tonnage to cover the cost. A similar plan was adopted for the planned cut from Bufferies Basin to Baptist End, the tramroad being of 2ft 4in gauge 'with proper turn offs with Wood Oak sleepers in a permanent . . . manner'.[17]

To begin with, considerable effort had to be devoted to fostering trade on the new route, and for some years the company strove to encourage it by example. In November 1797 Lord Dudley was approached to contract for a supply of coals from Park Head and Bumblehole collieries and was allowed to navigate coals from them into the old canal free of toll until the new extension was open. A year later, however, he still had not supplied any coal, and a further memorial had to be sent, followed by a deputation, after which a contract was signed. A sub-committee of four was set up to deal with sales in the Birmingham market and another, of two, for all other markets. Unfortunately, Lord Dudley was behindhand with his deliveries and disputes arose over the price, resulting in a modification of the contract so that, with certain exceptions, the company were to have all the coal raised at the two collieries for three years but the price was to be fixed at the end of each quarter by two referees 'taking into Consideration any extra allowance of weight made by other Coal Masters on the line of the Birmingham Canal'. The committee were 'induced to acquiesce in the above alterations' only 'out of great personal respect to Lord Dudley and from a firm reliance on his Lordships assurance, that every exertion [would] be made to raise all the Coals . . . that the nature of the Concerns will admit of'.[18] They were, nevertheless, selling the coal at twice the price they were paying at the end of 1801, when they had to cut the price 10 per cent to reduce stocks.

Advertisements were issued seeking carriers and offering them wharfs and warehouses while plans went ahead to erect the latter wherever trade could be anticipated and to find yet other sources of coal. When Messrs Sutton, Pearce and Danby of Halesowen wanted to commence in the carrying trade land was bought for a warehouse for them at the Worcester Canal junction, they were 'accomodated' with two or three boats and the company's agent was instructed to give 'every assistance . . . to promote the . . . undertaking. And that it be recommended to the Stourbridge Canal Committee to patronise & promote the same'.[19] It was decided to erect a warehouse at Bumblehole 'so soon as any responsible person will come forwards to take the same and pay a rent of $7\frac{1}{2}$ p^r C^t of the Money laid out'[20] and an agreement was made with the Stratford Canal whereby the two canals would each lend the Worcester Canal £400 to enable it to raise its banks from Selly Oak to King's Norton in order to promote trade.

Contracts were made to sell two boat-loads of lime weekly, from the company's Park Head kilns, to each of two carriers at 10s (50p) a ton plus 9d tonnage to Selly Oak and Messrs Scott, Green and Bennett (called 'the Committee residing in Birmingham') were rented a warehouse and crane on the wharf at Birmingham 'for the purpose of Establishing the Carriage of Merchandise along the Netherton line', they on their part agreeing 'not to Navigate any Coals to Birm^m but what are brought along the line of the Dudley Canal'.[21]

These measures were so successful that the company gave up its own trading at the end of 1803, though it continued to rely quite heavily on drawbacks on trade it wished to encourage—9d a ton out of 2s (10p) total on all coal coming through the old tunnel to the Netherton Canal, one shilling on all coal going to the Oxford Canal via King's Norton and Kingswood to oppose the allowance made by the Warwick Canals favouring the BCN—this latter combined with three months credit—6d (2½p) a ton on coal to Tardebigge or wharfs on the Stratford Canal, and many more. In 1810 a wharf and warehouse in Birmingham were rented to Danks & Co on condition that they navigated not less than 80 tons per week to Birmingham via Netherton or paid the tonnage, which was not to exceed that payable on the route via the old tunnel and the BCN (2s 2½d (11p) to Birmingham and 1s 7½d (8p) in the opposite direction). As a result of the growth of trade, by the end of 1810 James Sadler, the lock-keeper at Park Head, needed an assistant 'in making out the Tickets, Guaging the Boats, and regulating the passage of Boats'. Two years later the company appointed, at a salary of £250pa, a 'person... to superintend and promote the Trade and general Interests of the Concern'.[22] This was Thomas Brewin, himself concerned in the coal trade, a member of the committees of the Stratford and Stourbridge canals and later of the Stratford & Moreton Tramway. When the clerk died in 1824 he was given his post also, but at no increase in salary; it was not until 1838 that this was raised to £400, where it remained for the rest of the canal's separate history.

Markets improved when the Worcester & Birmingham Canal was opened to the Severn (1815) and the Stratford-upon-Avon Canal was completed throughout (1816), and finance improved with them. At the beginning of the century the clerk's salary had had to be reduced owing to lack of funds and the next year a

Special Assembly had to be called to empower borrowing of up to £10,000 to meet current deficits; there was £2,000 owing to Lord Dudley for coal, for which he was asked to wait two years, and tolls had to be collected fortnightly. Even as late as 1804 so much was owed to Shaw Hellier for coals that he gave the company's clerk notice to quit from his house (which happened to stand on Hellier's land) as a means of bringing pressure to bear.

However, by then the worst was over. In August 1804, 'It appearing . . . that there will be a sufficient Sum in the Treasurers hands',[23] a first dividend of £1 was paid and a similar sum was paid at varying intervals thereafter, usually six months but sometimes more, until growing trade raised it to £2 half yearly between 1824 and 1826, falling back to £1 in 1831 but after 1836 remaining fairly constant at between £2 and £2.50.

A major difficulty was that both the main tunnels—the 'Old Tunnel' and that at Lappal—were affected by mining subsidence and trade was constantly being interrupted. A further problem at first was the obstruction caused in the old tunnel by boats loading with limestone at the underground quarries but complaints about this died down in the new century, probably reflecting the effectiveness of new regulations. Congestion was not helped by boats using the tunnel out of hours, and the lock-keeper at Tipton was discharged for permitting this in July 1800 (though he was still there ten months later). Locked bars were put up to prevent entry. The practice developed of linking several boats together so that they could be taken through by the crew of one only which slowed down traffic in spite of attempts to speed it up, but the main trouble was the condition of the tunnels. It even became necessary to lay down as a general rule: 'In case of any Stoppages in the Lapal or the Old Dudley Canal Tunnels that our Clerk . . . do immediately inform the Trades thereof'[24] and at one time the committee were forced to admit that it would be useless to encourage the coal trade through the tunnel on account of its condition.

New by-laws for working through the tunnels were adopted

almost annually during the thirties and forties. A sub-committee was set up in 1836 to consider the matter of the Dudley tunnel and Brewin suggested an engine at Park Head, perhaps to serve in the way later used successfully at Lappal but perhaps only to maintain the water level; be that as it may, the engine currently in use, which was on hire from the trustees of the Earl of Dudley, was pronounced unfit for the purpose and another was purchased from them for £500. In 1839 a trial was made in the Gosty Hill tunnel of an 'Engine for the working of Boats thro' Tunnels' offered by a Mr Redmund. It turned out to be a steam boat which was 'not . . . equal to the work required'.[25]

The next year, just before a complaint from the BCN that the trade was being incommoded by the condition of the old tunnel, Brewin suggested that movement could be speeded by building three locks at Park Head to make a junction between the Dudley and Netherton canals (presumably to join Park Head to Bumblehole) at an estimated cost of £4,475. No more was heard of this, but two months later he produced a plan for working boats through the tunnels at a cost of £6,000 which was voted 'not desirable at present'. Instead it was decided to employ an engineer to survey the area between Dixons Green and Tipton 'with reference to the practicability of making a New communication by Tunnel in that direction', but with equal lack of result. In 1843 it was suggested that the passage of boats might be facilitated by 'Machineray', by cleansing or by the adoption of the scheme by then in use at Lappal but not long before the canal ceased its independent existence the problem was still there; tonnage was reduced on the line from Stourbridge via Selly Oak 'for the purpose of relieving the Old Dudley Tunnel from a part of the Trade' and yet another sub-committee was set up to consider how to remove 'the obstruction so much complained of'.[26]

Lappal was, if anything, worse. Hardly a year passed without some damage occurring. In 1801 the company owed Lord Dudley £1,800 for coals which they had been unable to sell because the tunnel was closed for two months and it was out of action for twice that period in 1805. The engineer was ordered at first to go through the tunnel once a week, but in 1806 this was increased to twice, he being allowed a shilling a week expenses, possibly for 'legging', and bricks were constantly kept stacked at the end of the tunnel to be ready for the next collapse. This was a problem that found no solution until the tunnel became permanently impassable in this century but in 1841 the speed of transit was improved when a pumping engine 'now at Coombes Wood' was removed to the end of the tunnel at a cost of £314 15s (£314.75). At the same time a stop-gate was installed. When traffic was travelling from west to east water was pumped from the west of the stop-gate to the east of it, creating a current in the tunnel and raising the water in the Selly Oak pound 6in; a paddle was then raised in the gate to allow the water to flow back and assist craft in the opposite direction. The time for passing the tunnel was reduced from three to two hours and Brewin was given £50 in plate for his 'contrivance'.

THE WYRLEY AND ESSINGTON CANAL

The last canal to appear in the coalfield was little bigger to begin with than the Dudley Canal and aroused little opposition, since it was merely a feeder into the Birmingham's Wolverhampton level. Even when extended it posed a threat which could easily be contained.

Notice of intention to apply for an Act appeared in August 1791, giving the route as 'from Wyrley thro Busbury to communicate with the Birm^m Canal at or near the Town of Wolverhampton' and representatives met the Committee of the Birmingham Canal to discuss the junction point[27] which, not surprisingly, the Birmingham committee wished to see at the summit rather than one lock down as suggested. When this point had been conceded by the new canal, at an estimated cost of £2,000, more trouble arose because the Bill included no safeguards for water. For some reason the solicitors for the new canal could not enter into any engagement respecting the security of the water and pressure had to be exerted by a deputation to London. It was successful, the Birmingham Canal being given the right to prevent passage whenever water in the new canal was less than 6in above that in the Wolverhampton level. In addition, 'the Weirs and other Works in & upon the upper & lower ponds of the said Intended Canal [were to] be so constructed that all the waste of surplus Water' flowed into the Birmingham Canal.[28] As a result of this agreement the Bill passed rapidly with no opposition and received the Royal Assent on 30 April 1792.[29] £25,000 could be raised in 200 shares and £20,000 in loans, with tonnage at 9d per ton for minerals whatever the distance and 2d per ton/mile for other goods.

Perhaps wishing to avoid the errors of their predecessors, the proprietors of the new canal decided not to begin cutting until the land was bought and to execute no part by contract except the cutting. The engineer was apparently W. Pitt,[30] possibly the Staffordshire historian and author of the *Survey of the Agriculture of Staffordshire* (1818), but the absence of committee minute books means that we have no information on the detailed progress of the works. The canal was open to the junction in November 1794, apart from the normal problem of the stop-lock. It was 28ft wide at top water, 16ft at the bottom and 4ft 6in deep.

In September 1794 the Birmingham committee, on one of their tours of inspection, found that the stop-lock 'consisted of two Gates only, constructed to prevent the Water flowing into the Birm^m Canal but not the contrary way'[31] and this remained the position until well into 1796, passage being prevented when the levels were wrong, which caused hardship and hard feelings. In April 1796 the Wyrley Canal agreed to erect another pair of gates 'or some other means' to protect the water and finally decided to model the lock on that at the Dudley Canal junction. When built, the lock leaked, which was felt to be inevitable 'whilst the waters of the Canals are so nearly upon a level' and so the gates were kept locked. The problem was reported solved at the end of the year, but as late as 1798 the Wyrley Canal's agent was accused of breaking the padlock to take a boat through when the water in his canal was '1½ Inches below the Birm^m Canal Water & the Lock

NEW CANALS, 1790-1830

Gates so leaking that the pumps were incapable of raising the Water in the Lock to the height requir'd'.[32] A deputation from the Wyrley Canal agreed to alter the lock and keep their water level higher. Absence of complaints suggests that the promise was kept.

By this time the canal had been considerably extended. It had been decided to apply for a Bill for this purpose as early as May 1793, only shortly after construction of the original canal had begun, and public notice was given in August. The new route was to join the Coventry Canal at Huddlesford, between Fradley and Whittington Brook, providing an alternative, and shorter, route for Tipton coals to the Trent and southwards and thus directly affecting the Birmingham Canal. The latter were, however, bought off by a compensation toll of 3d per ton on all coal going from Wolverhampton to Fazeley by the new route and the Act[33] received the Royal Assent on 28 March 1794 without opposition.

It permitted an extension from Birchills to Huddlesford with a branch from Catshill to Rushall (the Hay Head branch) and provided for the necessary money to be raised, £75,000 by new shares whose purchasers would be united with the old proprietors in one company, and another £40,000 by loans or calls as necessary. In fact the old proprietors bought many of the shares. The old shareholders were to have 5 per cent interest until the new canal was complete and thereafter 5 per cent extra dividend. Once again tonnage was fixed by lump sum rather than mileage for minerals; 2s (10p) per ton from below Catshill lock to Huddlesford, 9d on the main line if not passing Catshill lock and 1s 3d (6p) if it was passed. Other goods were again 2d per ton/mile. The new canal could not take water from mills and other canals nor send too much overflow into Whittington Brook because of possible damage to the Marquess of Donegall's pleasure gardens.

The first Assembly of the new company decided, in view of the existing premium on the old shares, to create 600 new shares, 200 to be allocated free of all calls to the old proprietors and 400 to be sold at £125 per share—thus raising £50,000 while creating

£75,000 of liabilities. At this time there were 43 old proprietors listed and they were joined by 88 new ones. Work began immediately, but the unusual course was followed that the proprietors paid for everything 'other than the cutting and completing the Canal Towing Path Bridges Locks and Lockhouses' out of their own pockets, in proportion to their holdings. This included 'Land for Wharfs and the making the same and also all Collateral Cuts Basons, Reservoirs Engines and all other Works and Conveniences'.[34]

Calls were imposed only on new shares but in June 1796, when the new shareholders had paid £100 per share, it was decided that, since this was 'equal to what the Original Proprietors have or will expend in respect of the Original Canal', all distinctions should cease and 'the whole Eight hundred Shares became Consolidated and made one Concern'[35] with future calls on all equally. Nevertheless, as late as November 1797 attempts were being made 'to settle the Accounts between the Canal and Extensions'. It appeared that some 'old proprietors' had a considerable balance in the hands of the treasurer, so it was decided to give them £7 per share, the rest of the balance, totalling £562 16s 4d (£562.81½), being 'paid over to the joint and consolidated Concern, which shall pay all Demands whatsoever'.[36]

By this time there were the financial troubles typical of all concerns at this period and a running battle was fought with proprietors who defaulted on calls. At one stage they included the clerk, but he remained in office. In April 1798 it was reported impossible to complete the Hay Head branch for lack of funds, but by some means resources were found and the canal was complete, apart from the Hay Head branch, by April 1799, advertisements in the Oxford, Coventry, Hull and Gainsborough papers showing the role planned for the canal as a means of access to distant markets. £1,000 was borrowed to complete the Hay Head branch in May 1801, but it was reported still not complete a year later.

In July 1800 a special meeting was requisitioned by five proprietors who had seen a statement that the company was owed

£3,120 by defaulting proprietors, 'as there must have been great Neglect somewhere to have allowed so large a Balance to remain due'. The decision was reached, however, with fourteen present, 'that the Conduct of the Committee has been such as to merit the Approbation of the Company present', even though it was revealed that orders to proceed against defaulters had not been complied with. Four months later the company declared its first dividend of £2 per share. The crisis was over and the defaulters gradually paid up. By May 1803 the committee were being thanked 'for their present attention to the prosperity of the concern'.[37]

Like those of the neighbouring canals, the Wyrley & Essington proprietors engaged in the carrying trade, commencing in 1794, the necessary money being at first borrowed from the treasurer. Two years later another £5,000 was borrowed for this purpose amongst others and the committee were empowered to contract with Vernon, who was at that time their chairman, for up to one hundred tons daily of large coals at 4s 6d (22½p) per ton and twenty tons daily of slack at 2s 6d (12½p). Six months later the unusual device was adopted of a £3 call, as and when the committee thought fit, 'to be applied by them as a fund ... for the sole purpose of providing a Trade upon the Canal'. Apparently the venture was not successful, or it aroused too much opposition, for a mere two months later the Committee of Trade was ordered 'not to proceed fur^r in carrying Coals or in anything relative to the Business of Trade'; three weeks later it was decided to rent out the company's boats. Six years later it was decided to use 'the growing Profits and Monies arising from the Tonnage' to establish a trade in coal, lime and limestone 'until such time as the Mines of Coal and Lime Rocks upon the Canal are so worked as to render such interference unecessary' but the outcome is unrecorded.[38] A suggestion was also made that the drawbacks might encourage through trade but against a note of the only one agreed (of 3d per ton on all coal taken beyond Huddlesford) is noted 'not done'.

One reason for the paucity of trade was very probably the state of the canal. Leakages into the mines were a cause of complaint in January 1800 and 'The first Boat that came up the Locks with Ore in June 1801 . . . stop'd for want of water in Lock pounds'.[39] Next month it was claimed that there was water for boats carrying 18 tons, but the very next day two boatmen with exactly that load complained of want of water and alleged they had been two days coming from Lichfield.

Matters had not been made easier by a disaster in the middle of 1799 when the embankment of the Cannock Heath reservoir gave way

> and the water swept everything before it in the line it took through Shenstone Hopwas, Drayton &c till it fell into and overflooded the Tame at Tamworth. At Blackbrook, seven miles from the reservoir the new stone bridge was blown up; numbers of sheep and some cattle were drowned . . . The damage sustained is . . . calculated at many thousand pounds. At Hammerswich, near Lichfield, the meadows are twelve inches deep with the Gravel the Water brought down.[40]

Later the damage was said to have been exaggerated and the canal to be completely navigable, but the result must have been an increased water shortage.

As if all this were not enough the company were plagued with a dispute with their leading proprietor which seemed to defy solution. Henry Vernon was the largest coalowner in the district through which the canal passed and, as we have seen, was for some time the chairman of the company. In 1798 he was clearly suffering from severe water shortage, for the utmost that could be promised in the Essington Wood summit, where his mines were situated, was enough water for 15-ton boats, and that only for three weeks in July, during which period Vernon was paid for pumping water into the canal. Eighteen months later Vernon petitioned Parliament for a Bill to permit him to by-pass the canal by means of a railway from Essington to the Staffs & Worcs Canal at Little Sandon. Both canals opposed him, the Wyrley Canal alleging that he had become bankrupt in 1789 and had handed administration of his lands over to Hordern. The canal had been

Page 67 (*above*) Two centuries of wear under the lock-beam, Farmer's Bridge flight; (*below*) the east portal of Lappal tunnel, 1950, with Ward's Brickworks wharf on the right. This was filled in and built over, 1971–2

Page 68 (*above*) Smethwick locks, the originals on the left, Smeaton's duplicates on the right. In the extreme right foreground is the parapet of the towing-path bridge over the feeder from Rotten Park reservoir (1972); (*below*) three canal levels from Brass-house Lane bridge near Smethwick: the first cutting in the middle with the Telford cutting and Galton bridge to the left and the first summit, now a footpath (marked by two figures) on the right. The building used to house a pumping engine

built in reliance on the carriage of his coals. The treasurer (the same Hordern) lent £3,000 for the purpose of opposing the Bill. Deputations were sent to Vernon and to his friends for their assistance in dissuading him and Telford was commissioned to report on the state of the canal. Eventually the Bill was deferred by an agreement, ratified in May 1799, whereby Hordern was to retain £3,000 'out of the Trust Monies he is empowered to retain under a certain Article Dated the 14th day of March 1792 made between Mr. Vernon and Mr. Hordern', and pay it to the company in part discharge of sums the company had spent or would spend according to the Article 'or for Mr. Vernon's private Accomodation'.[41] This is the first mention of this trust fund in the surviving records but it appears to have originated when the canal was first proposed and was to ensure Vernon's access to it, including presumably his private branch. The money in the fund was provided by Vernon who promised also to carry all his coals by the canal. The agreement appears to have covered also a branch railway to the canal, for the casting of rails and commencement of construction were ordered in June.

Vernon was certainly not in a conciliatory mood, however, despite the agreement. In May, having been refused permission to drain the canal to raise a sunken boat, he cut the bank through and lowered a mile-and-a-half pound 7in. When the railway was built he did not approve of it 'in as much as there are no pass byes . . . & that such Railway was not carried to the Centre of the Collieries'.[42]

In December 1799 it was agreed to submit differences to arbitration, but it was some time before agreement could be reached as to the arbitrators, the committee meanwhile demanding that Hordern pay them the money they had spent

> in cutting and executing a certain branch of Canal from a place called Whitmores Meadow to Mr. Vernons new Engine and called Mr. Vernons branch . . . together with the expence of erecting the Engine at Mr. Vernons Old Colliery and all such other Sums of Money as may have been expended for his sole use.[43]

Nevertheless the dispute dragged on, though the paucity of

records makes it difficult to see exactly what was happening. In August 1803, for example, the committee were still assuring Vernon that they had 'the strongest wish to settle all matters in dispute with him upon the most liberal Terms',[44] but three months later they laid it down that no agreement was to be made with him in future unless in writing signed by both parties. The last we see is an order of May 1812, reiterated twelve months later, to commence proceedings to recover the balance due from him.

The same dearth of records referred to earlier makes it difficult to depict the activity of the concern, except that it can be said to have thriven in a quiet way. In 1820, however, discussions began with the BCN on 'the expediency & propriety of a consolidation of the Interests of the two Undertakings'[45]—a consolidation which would be securely based in their complementary nature, as well in the matter of water supply as of traffic. At this date the canal was in good repair, with a fine reservoir, and paid a 6 per cent dividend; trade, however, had been 'hitherto very limited', which raised the possibility of a rate-cutting war between the two concerns. Unfortunately the terms offered by the BCN at this time were considered so 'inadequate' that the Wyrley & Essington broke off discussions.

It was the problem of a physical junction between the canals which next raised the matter. In November 1822 a sub-committee had been set up to investigate the cause of the decline in tonnage, 'to inquire what new Avenues and Channels of Trade may be opened—What are the best Means of using our surplus water— What Communication it would be prudent and practicable to make with other contiguous and collateral Canals'[46]—all questions which pointed in the direction of the BCN. Two years later, while rejecting the price offered them for that water, the Wyrley Canal asked for 'an opportunity of convincing the Birmigham Canal Com^{tee} of the value of their concern arising from prospects of very increased Trade which are likely to be permanent & profitable'.[47] This time, however, it was the Wyrley Canal's proposal— to rank the shares of each equally (there were at this time, 4,000 BCN shares)—that was unacceptable.

The next year a survey was made 'as to the eligibility and the practicability of making any Extensions or Improvements',[48] against a background of suggestions from coalowners and others that the two canals should be linked at Walsall. Since neither canal took any steps towards effecting this a new company was proposed

> for making, constructing and maintaining a Navigable Cut or Canal from or near to a certain street lane or place called Walmer Lane otherwise Lancaster street in the parish of Saint Martin in Birmingham . . . to and into the navigation called the Wyrley and Essington Canal at or near to a place called the Birchills[49]

—together with another link from the Wyrley Canal to the Staffs & Worcs Canal near Otherton. This received little support and was followed a year later by an equally unsuccessful proposal for a 'Birmingham, Walsall and Liverpool Junction Canal'. At this stage the BCN set up a sub-committee to consider the question of a junction.

The report of this sub-committee stated that such a junction would be 'inexpedient' unless there was a compensation toll of at least 1s 4d (6½p) per ton for all goods using the junction to enter the Wyrley Canal since the main effect would be to attract Tipton coals to distant markets via the Wyrley Canal. Little would come the other way since the coals on the Wyrley line were sulphurous and little in demand; the best measure would be to concentrate on keeping the trade in its existing channels by lowering the summit. On their part the Wyrley Canal employed Provis to survey the line of a possible junction; he offered three alternative routes but agreement could not be reached with the BCN.

Two years later the mineowners tried again, petitioning both canals, and in 1830 the Wyrley Canal yet again proposed union. Negotiations dragged on, listlessly and fruitlessly, until 1832, only to be revived in 1835 when a junction was suggested either at Walsall or with the Anson branch. A year later the BCN were surveying a line for a junction but just then a diversion occurred;

it was realised that surplus water from the Wyrley Canal was not being discharged into the Wolverhampton level as required in the Act. Legal advice was taken and the Wyrley Canal built a new weir, but it did not prove satisfactory and complaints were renewed.

Events now began to move faster. Following renewed deputations the BCN agreed to build the Walsall link providing the Wyrley Canal made the necessary water available, and set up yet another sub-committee to consider union. It was then discovered that the surplus water was still going elsewhere and negotiations were broken off.

Pressure from mineowners was, however, now very strong, as there were new mines waiting to be opened in the area. The Wyrley Canal suggested a union on the basis of a guaranteed dividend of £6 in 1838, rising to £9 in 1841, each share in the two concerns to rank equally thereafter. This seemed attractive to the BCN who hoped to divert some of the Farmer's Bridge traffic through this route, but they could not agree to the terms. Relations were not helped at this point by an attempt on the part of the Wyrley Canal to pass water through the Wolverhampton level to supply the Dudley Canal and by their sale of 1,000 locksful to the Birmingham & Liverpool Junction Canal, but public pressure was kept up, public meetings being held in Walsall and deputations sent to the committees. At the end of 1838 a Bill for a Walsall Junction Canal was promoted and forced the hand of the Birmingham Canal who agreed to build the junction provided the Wyrley Canal supplied the water.

Negotiations now proceeded as to how much should be paid on each Wyrley Canal share before it could be considered the equivalent of one in the Birmingham Canal, agreement finally being reached at £49, with 4 per cent interest to be deducted from the dividend if it was not paid and both companies to declare an equal dividend of £5 in June 1839. When this was put to a Special Assembly of the Birmingham Canal it was urged in its favour that it would dispel fear of injury from the Walsall line and 'lessen the chances of interference with the Mineral Districts'.[50]

The Bill for the merger was introduced with the Tame Valley Bill but dropped when the latter aroused opposition. However, the Walsall link was included and was commenced as soon as the Act received the Royal Assent.[51] The Act for a union of the two canals followed a year later[52] and the junction was opened in March 1841: 'the local trader will be relieved, the voyage to Autherley quickened, and the conveyance of heavy commodities from the Walsall Level to the Trent, much facilitated'.[53] One wonders why it had taken so long.

CHAPTER 4

Improving the Birmingham Canal, 1778–1818

WHILE the canal system of the area was being extended in the manner related it was not to be expected that the BCN itself would remain unchanged. Indeed improvements and extensions were a permanent feature of its life from the beginning, though certain periods were particularly hectic.

One matter which was always requiring attention was that of water supply.[1] Natural sources were never adequate; mining caused abundant leakages and the local streams were already pre-empted for mills. Even before Smeaton reported on the problem in 1782 two-thirds of the water was provided by pumping engines, and his suggestion was adopted that 'what supplies the two-thirds may just as well supply the other third'.[2] Much of this water was pumped out of the mines by the mineowners and thus does not concern us here, but a considerable amount was provided by the activities of the canal company itself.

The first engines to be installed were recirculatory—ie they returned water used as lockage to the top of the locks—and this was always the purpose of the majority of the engines. When Brindley had recommended locks instead of a tunnel at Smethwick he had suggested recirculating the water by means of a 'Fire Engine' but it was not until August 1776, however, that Mr Henn, the Chairman, was asked 'to have some conversations with Mr. Boulton about the Erecting of a Fire Engine upon that part of the Canal between the Third Lock and Shenstones Mill to raise the

Water Eighteen Feet'.[3] It was to be sited between the seventh and eighth locks—ie between the top lock and the one below at Spon Lane—and was complete and working by April 1778, at a cost of £1,706.[4] It was so successful that another was forthwith ordered and installed at Smethwick; for some reason it was considerably cheaper (£1,290). 'Superintending of Spon Lane Engine' cost £19 in the six months to September 1779, and coals £41 2s 8½d (41.13½), the new engine requiring £25 16s 5d (£25.82) for 'Attendance Suet Candles & C' and £50 18s 1½d (£50.90½) for coals.[5]

The success of these two engines encouraged the company to consider a similar engine at the end of the Ocker Hill branch, extending eastwards from the Coseley Loop, to pump up water from the Broadwaters level, which was then under construction. A tunnel was made into the side of the hill from the lower level and a pit sunk to it for the pump. It was ready by the end of 1785, but required considerable attention because of the liability of the tunnel to subside as a result of mining operations in the vicinity— a constant hazard to all canal works in this area.

The sides and bottom of the branch fell into Mr Wood's workings in February 1795, making the branch unusable while the canal on the lower level was undermined by Messrs Wall and Danks. Soon after Wood undermined the tunnel as well and all three were presented at the Assizes. Nearly two years later the floor of the engine pit sank 2ft and a visit to Wood's pit revealed not only that coal had been got from under the tunnel and canal, being 'for abt 200 Yards in length . . . at present supported by Pillars', but that part of the workings were on fire. This would probably destroy some of the pillars and Wood planned to take away the rest.[6] The committee refused to plan another tunnel but decided to await the collapse and charge Wood. Apparently this gave him stay because it was the end of this particular threat, though eighteen months later a Mr Hawkes had to be forced to desist from getting ironstone under the tunnel. Two years later yet another group of coalowners, Messrs Banks, Read and Dumaresq, were getting coal under the branch, followed soon after by renewed information from Wood that he was proceeding to mine under the engine-house itself. 'It having been the general opinion that there is a fault in the Mine under the said Engines', it was decided to investigate.[7] Two years later negotiations began to buy the mines under the engine-house; Mr Bagnall, who was responsible for working these pits, was informed of his legal liability for damage, to which he replied that 'of this . . . he was aware And that the Amount of the damage a breach might occasion . . . would probably exceed the Amount of the Property of all the Persons concern'd in the Coal Mine'.[8] He and the company's engineer were left to work out the surface area of the mine to be left unworked and it was decided that an area of 36yd radius from the engine-house would be suitable. Bagnall also agreed to pay half the cost of a new tunnel and water course in case the old fell in and it was contracted for at 15s (75p) 'per Yard forward where it is capable of being worked with a pike & to allow a reasonable compensation for such parts as may require Gunpowder'.[9] It was completed and water let in on 3 April 1805. In its turn it had to be protected by purchasing the mines below.

This seemed to solve this problem, but ten years later there was a complaint that the engines created such a current that it was difficult to get boats out '& that when the Cut is crowded with Boats they cannot be haled out without the Engines being stopped working', the engines themselves being damaged by 'small Coaks & other filth drawn up by the strength of the Current of Water'.[10] A new cut was suggested and an estimate received (£249) but it was decided to do nothing pending the introduction of a 'mudding machine' to dredge the cut. However a new cut was built on the higher level at a cost of £367 to boat coal round the back of the engine-house to save the expense of breakages of coal in wheeling it round.

As will be clear from some of the quotations above, by this time the original engine alone had long been inadequate for its tasks. The work it had to do was greatly increased in 1790 when the company began to pump from Broadwaters (see below) and, after some initial wavering, the committee decided to instal another engine of the same power as the old. The new pit was ready in February 1791 and the new engine was apparently working at the beginning of March. By the middle of 1802, however, new coal pits at Gospel Oak and Bradley Hall were so increasing the traffic through the locks at Riders Green and Spon Lane as to necessitate a third engine. Boulton & Watt were again called in and asked to have it working by May 1803. They recommended a new boiler and offered to supply an engine with 46in cylinder and 8ft stroke for £1,460, the company providing the pumping equipment. By August 1802 the drawings were ready and the foundations were being prepared; the engine was working by the time required.

Even with this boost, by 1809 the engines were incapable of returning all the water which fell into the Willinsworth (lower) level and water was 'daily running waste out of it'. This was made worse on occasions such as that in 1812 when one of the engines was recylindered; the remaining two were inadequate to their task and water had constantly to be drawn out of the reservoir on the Wyrley & Essington Canal—and paid for.

Meanwhile there had been changes at Smethwick in consequence of lowering the summit. The Spon Lane engine had been sold to the Dudley Canal—though not before consideration of its resiting to supply the locks at Toll End, Bradley Hall and Gospel Oak (the latter never built)—and the Smethwick engine had been supplied with a larger pump, the original one being used for the second engine at Ocker Hill. By 1804 the Smethwick engine-house and tunnel needed replacement at an estimated cost of £950. The question of whether, instead, the old should be repaired or whether the engine as well should be replaced, was referred to Boulton & Watt. Since they offered a new engine for £1,146 this was agreed, the pump to be of 34in diameter (as compared with 24in originally and 30in when the summit was lowered). After some problems about payment which led to delays in delivery the engine began working on 9 May 1805.

Once the Warwick & Birmingham Canal was open the increased use of the locks at Farmer's Bridge made renewed demands upon the water supply and the success of the existing engines led to suggestions of another to pump water from Ashted locks to the Hospital Pond at their top. In 1808 the engineer was asked for the costs of pumping water at Smethwick and Ocker Hill and he reported them as $2\frac{1}{4}$d and $3\frac{1}{2}$d per lock respectively, with an extra 2d in each case for capital charges at 8 per cent. At this time Rennie was making a survey of the canal and Watt and Galton, in their comments on his report, stated that it appeared 'that in any possible case a Reservoir of considerable magnitude [was] necessary—considering the returning of the Water by Engine from the Digbeth Level as a more expensive and uncertain Method'. 'In this opinion,' we are told, 'the Majority of the Gentlement present concur[red]'.[11] There were, however, problems in the way of finding a site for the reservoir and it was finally decided that an engine was the answer, with a reservoir 3ft deep to take the overflow at the bottom of the locks, this to include the 'commencement of a Canal some time ago proposed to be made from the Digbeth lower pond upon a Level to the Canal at Ashton Brook'.[12] Two engines were proposed to raise seventy locksful in eighteen hours. Two engines were accordingly ordered but a deputation was sent from the Warwick & Birmingham Canal complaining that they paid $4\frac{1}{2}$d per ton as compensation for lockage water at Digbeth and requesting this be reduced if the water were to be pumped back. In any case, they claimed, they would suffer injury—but legal opinion confirmed the right of the BCN to the water. Meanwhile a site was reported on the lower level which could serve as a reservoir for up to 300 locksful of mines engine water 'to be raised as wanted into the Summit by Ocker Hill Engines' and thus obviate the need for a new engine.

However, an apparently final decision to instal one engine was made in April 1811 and, because of the high cost of land for reservoirs, an estimate was requested of the cost of another engine to raise the water a further stage from the Hospital Pond to the summit. Further discussions were held with the Warwick Canal and the Ashted engine began pumping at the end of September

1812, its tunnel draining in the process forty-four local wells, each of which cost £8.50 to deepen. A report was made on raising the water further, Watt suggesting

> that the best means of conveying Water from the Hospital Pond to the upper level at Birmingham would be to drive a Tunnel from Snow Hill to the three Arch Bridge & erect an Engine there which may be so constructed as to raise the Water out of the Hospital Pond into the Branch of Canal belonging to Mr. James & from thence through Iron Pipes into the upper Level, near the Albion Mill,[13]

but the project was allowed to remain in abeyance.

Long before this, however, the company had begun to use engines to supply itself with water as well as to recirculate it. This policy was adopted in 1788, in conjunction with the extension to Broadwaters on what became, ultimately, the Walsall level. At this time the Smethwick summit was being lowered and the company's engineers were ordered 'to make the best enquiries they can as to the depths of the Pitts and Hollows at Broadwater in order to determine ... the propriety of removing [the Spon Lane Engine] or the erection of a new and more powerful one, to raise the water out of the Hollows'.[14] This was not done however and an engine was ordered from Wilkinson, to be built under the supervision of Boulton & Watt, to pump water from disused mines at Broadwaters into the new level. The new engine was working by the beginning of 1790. It was even suggested, but not agreed, that surplus water from the summit could be run into these mines for storage. At the beginning of 1804, however, £40 was approved for a feeder for surplus water from the summit to Broadwater hollows, with raised banks there to enable more water to be stored, which suggested that the land had sunk and provided water storage also on the surface—as it did until utilised as a tip in the 1960s. The feeder was already conveying surplus water by the end of January 1804.

However, no such source of water could be considered reliable for ever in a mining area. In November 1806 the committee were informed that the proprietors of mines in the Broadwaters area intended to work them and that it would be necessary to drain the pool. Although some delay occurred, by 1811 the mineowners were building a sough for that purpose. Close watch was kept, legal opinion was sought and the committee decided to apply for an injunction which was granted in January of 1812. Flushed with victory the committee proceeded to order the blocking of the sough, but were prevented by physical opposition. Renewed application to Chancery ensued and the injunction was overturned because damages should have been sought first. Following unsuccessful mediation by Mr Fereday and failure at Stafford Assizes (when not one special juryman turned up) negotiations began with Samuel Lloyd, representing the 'heirs of Parkes' who were building the sough. Eventually it was agreed to stop the sough so that the company could take the water, the mineowners agreeing not to drain the pool—except after heavy rains beyond the capacity of the company's engine—until they had erected at their own expense an engine powerful enough to pump the water back to the Walsall level. The sough was stopped up on 20 March 1813 but, once the mineowners had installed their engine, the company's engine at Broadwaters became redundant. In 1814 discussion began on a proposal to pump water at James Green and the next year it was decided to move the Broadwaters engine there, but the order was rescinded pending consultations with the Worcester & Birmingham Canal. Renewed plans were made in 1818, at which time there were also arguments with the heirs of Parkes about the poor state of repair of the sough, but the engine was finally sold to Sir Horace St Paul in 1819 for £900.

A similar exercise was mounted at Caponfield at the request of mineowners who wanted to work the thick coal which was surrounded by the flooded old workings of Wednesbury, Tipton and Bilston. They offered half the working expenses if the company erected the engine. It was agreed to instal an engine of the same size as those at Ocker Hill (later increased to 54in cylinder for which Boulton & Watt tendered £3,650). Originally it was intended to instal this at Barbon, with another at Caponfield, but the foundations were better at the latter place and the first engine began work on 19 March 1813. A reliable supply of water appeared ensured, although it proved difficult to persuade the mineowners to pay their share, and recourse had to be had to the law.

Even this, however, 'upon which so much reliance was placed' was diminished by new mining, and at the end of September 1820 it was exhausted. Other sources were sought but such were the vagaries of a mining area that at the beginning of 1822 the company was being asked to restart the engines to prevent neighbouring mines being drowned out, while eighteen months later it was reliably reported 'that Miners are now engaged in the working the Coal in such a manner as will draw all the Water out of Capponfield Pond before the next Season'.[15] Other sources were therefore suggested, including reservoirs at Rotton Park and Walsall and improvements in the reservoir belonging to the Wyrley Canal on Cannock Heath. Ironically, the owners of the mines drowned out by the draining of Caponfield asked the company to aid by setting up an engine! By January 1824, however, the engines were back at work, though there was now no summer supply, and the company considered selling the engines and contracting with mineowners in the area. The latter suggested they raise water to the surface and the Caponfield engines raise it the rest. It was finally decided to move one engine to Ocker Hill, but to keep the other. This, too, was sold in 1833.

Not surprisingly, when the area was hit by a 'very extraordinary & almost unparallel'd Drought', in 1826 it 'produced a State of difficulty such as was never experienced before'. £9,090 was spent on water, including £3,000 to the Wyrley Canal, the situation being accentuated by the even worse state of neighbouring canals, so that, for example, 'the Stratford Boats . . . were under the necessity of passing through the locks at Farmers Bridge and along the War^k Canal to Kingswood'. Caponfield provided only 4,000 locksful as opposed to 65,000 from mines engines, though the latter 'being frequently disused for a time, are seldom kept in a perfect state of Repair and cannot be put to work quickly, without considerable exertion, and great expense'. It was decided it was better to have 'Stock of Water on hand, sufficient for all the purposes of the Canal'.[16]

Thus was raised again the question which had been with the canal from the beginning, that of reservoirs. The original canal had two reservoirs at Smethwick, the 'great' which held 1,514 locksful but leaked and the 'lesser' which held 100, and another at Titford, holding 500, a total of three weeks supply. The result of Smeaton's report was to direct attention elsewhere. The only addition made was a small reservoir on Birmingham Heath and it was not until 1806 that it was agreed to make the Smethwick reservoir watertight. A few months later Rennie advised enlarging the Titford reservoir and building new ones in the Titford valley, and plans were produced for two new reservoirs in the 'Valleys above Oldbury', one of forty acres to hold 5,479 locksful at a cost of £2,902 and another of sixteen acres to hold 1,697 locksful at a cost of £1,386. The next year it was decided to proceed with a 70-acre site on the Row Brook, near Oldbury. The project hung fire for two years, and then land was found to be at between £300 and £400 the acre, so the question tended to merge into that of the advisability of a new engine at Digbeth. It appeared a reservoir was still necessary, however, and, a plan for one at Smethwick, to cover fifty acres at a cost of £3,268, having fallen through because the ground would not hold water, attention reverted to Row Brook. It was, however, finally abandoned in favour of the Ashted engine and reservoirs were not again considered until the time of Telford.

Improvements to the line of the canal usually had as their aim improved service to 'the Trade', but they, too, were often designed with water supply in mind. The first in time was of this type, when the bottom lock at Autherley, always a costly one in terms of water, was replaced by two shallower ones. There seems, in fact, no adequate reason why it was built at all. A reservoir was suggested just to supply it, and may actually have been built, but there is no sign of it now. Later a 'side lock' (presumably a side pound) was proposed, but the only real solution was early seen to be replacement. A survey was ordered when the Staffs & Worcs

IMPROVING THE BIRMINGHAM CANAL, 1778–1818

Canal was stopped for a month for repairs in 1775 and land was acquired, but it was not replaced until it needed repairing in 1784. It was by-passed by a 'Waggon Road' while the change took place. Cary[17] says the extra lock was built above the previous twentieth lock and it is true that the present-day bottom lock (now the twenty-first) is in a cutting, as if the top had been cut off and the earth cut away. Moreover, the lock above it has a single bottom gate, as was fashionable in 1784, but the bottom lock has mitre gates, as if in its original form. Nevertheless the canal takes a sharp turn above the twentieth lock, and there are traces of what could be a channel continuing the line from the nineteenth lock to join the Staffs & Worcs Canal some hundred yards further west. Cary wrote just after the event, and was probably right, but this channel presumably had some purpose, perhaps in connection with the lost reservoir.

A more sizeable problem was that of the summit, and its solution inaugurated a programme of improvement and renewal second only to the changes made by Telford thirty years later. The company was so thriving, however, that they were eventually able to finance the improvements out of profits, even though only after the initial accumulation of debts which took twenty years to pay off.

The summit was only about a thousand yards long and was subject to traffic jams at each end after the expansion of trade brought about by the Broadwaters extension. In 1786 the committee recommended to the General Assembly, who agreed, that 'the Cutting down the Smethwick Summit to the Level of the Wolverhampton Pond wou'd be attended with great publick utility'.[18] Smeaton was called in as engineer, but seems to have played little part, the work being done by the company's engineers. It was agreed to borrow up to £50,000, contracts were let and it was decided to build a second set of locks parallel to the old at the Smethwick end. The lock cottages were taken down and the materials used to build new ones at Tipton and Broadwaters.

The method of constructing the new canal was ingenious. In June it was reported that a new Canal twelve feet below the present course thro' the Smethwick Summit will in a very few days be made navigable, when it is proposed to carry away by the Boats returning to the Collieries a large quantity of the Soil necessary to be removed previous to the Navigation's being made still Six feet lower—such Soil to be used in raising and strengthening the Banks of the Canal which have been damaged by the working of the Coal Mines.[19]

The local newspaper deduced from this that

> That stupendous work now carrying on by the proprietors upon the Navigation . . . is at this time so far advanced that we understand the water will be let into its new course within a very few days. So vast and seemingly impracticable an undertaking has, we believe, never before been attempted in this kingdom; mountains have been raised and levelled, and canal of a well's depth, has been cut almost under canal . . . Three hundred labourers employed in the business, some in digging, some in filling, and the greater part in wheeling, in succession, up the declinity, for a mile in extent, their loaded barrows upon the stages effected for them, presents to the spectator a most pleasing, busy and novel scene.[20]

The water was drawn out of this new level in March of the next year and the new canal opened on 6 April, at a cost of £24,826. The redundant three locks at each end were filled, those at Spon Lane being brought to the light of day for the last time in July 1969 by a drag line excavator, which destroyed them in preparing the ground for a motorway.

This was the greatest single improvement in the line carried out in the first half-century of its existence. Even today, dwarfed by Telford's cutting and the Galton bridge, it is impressive. In its time it must have seemed a marvel and its effect in speeding the traffic was considerable. Moreover, by creating a summit level 15 miles long it greatly eased water supply problems; the proprietors must have considered it was money well spent.

Other improvements varied upwards from short branches of a few yards made to accommodate collieries—many of which, such as the Jesson and Ison arms, retain to this day the names of the mineowners who caused them to be built. Because the canal was built to carry coal first and foremost many more substantial extensions were also made to accommodate collieries. The Toll End branch, for example, included in the 1783 Act, was begun at the request of Messrs Dudley and Finch, coalowners who intended opening a new field. They asked for it to be suspended in May 1784 and it was reactivated at the request of Messrs Dixon and Amphlett eight years later. Others began to see its value and a deputation arrived from coalowners on the land above, requesting locks, which meant water had to be found. This was agreed, but estimates for the locks were not received until July 1797 and the extension was not complete until midsummer 1801, after several mineowners had complained of the delays.

In 1806 the extra traffic on the lower level made a new connection with the summit necessary and an investigation was ordered into the possibility of extending the original two locks by a further flight to the upper level. An estimate of £5,000 was produced and it was resolved to consider it 'at some future opportunity'. This soon came; a fortnight later it was agreed to build the connection, but it was more than a year later before Rennie's plans were available, only to be rejected in favour of a cheaper, shorter line from the company's engineer. The Toll End Communication Canal was opened in January 1809 to join the bottom of the Tipton Green locks which had been built to meet it. However, the upper lock was so constructed that boats could not pass 'into or out of such Lock without difficulty or without hindrance to the passage of Boats upon the Summit'[21] and it had to be altered. Further the Communication Canal leaked and had to be closed for repairs, not being finally opened until June, the contractor being allowed an extra £40 'in consideration of its being more difficult than could be expected.' At least at first the same tolls were charged on the route through these locks as if the boats had come the long way round. All these locks are now (1972) disused and dewatered, Tipton Green locks and Toll End Junction being filled in.

The number of branches built off the Broadwaters extension is an indication of the heavy traffic from the developing coal-field.

The Gospel Oak branch had also been included in the 1783 Act, but postponed at the request of local landowners. It was also reactivated by request in 1791 and was approved on an estimate of £1,099. Work began as soon as winter was over, with the intention of completing by November 1792. It was intended at this stage that the branch would end in some locks and there appears to have been some trouble arising from this for they were not built in April 1794. Six months later they were abandoned because of decisions relating to Bradley Hall, but the branch was not completed, as a level cut costing only £206, until six years later.

The Bradley Hall Extension left the main canal only a few hundred yards from that to Gospel Oak. It had been under discussion for some time, but was only finally approved in November 1794, when the cost with three locks, which could be supplied with water from the mines, was estimated at £1,383, as opposed to £1,338 on the level. Four locks were planned but three eventually built, the local mineowners being told that they were a replacement for those at Gospel Oak, though it was not until 1798 that arbitration was completed in proceedings to indemnify against claims resulting from the change. The locks are still (1972) in position, though dewatered. In 1849 another six were added above to join up with the Gospel Oak Loop Line (the old Main Line round Coseley Hill). This junction is now derelict and partly filled in.

All these could be carried out under powers given in existing Acts, but this was not the case with other plans which became linked with the Broadwaters extension. When first built, almost as a by-product of the Fazeley Canal, and under authorisation of the same Act, it was merely a short canal, leaving the Old Wednesbury Canal by a flight of eight locks down at Riders Green and proceeding on the level for about two miles to serve the collieries below Ocker Hill. Then, in 1790, a Mr Loxdale requested its extension on the same level 'into a large tract of valuable Coal Mines in the Valley between Darlaston and Bilston'.[22] A year later the Assembly decided to apply for a Bill to cover this and a cut from Winson Green to Soho. The land was surveyed, an estimate of £7,423 being produced, and Loxdale informed he would be charged 4d a ton for the new extension—later reduced to 2d plus engine water. Smeaton was asked to act as engineer.

Just before this an advertisement had appeared giving notice that the Wyrley & Essington company intended applying for powers to join their canal to the Birmingham by a line from Pool Hays to Broadwaters and at a meeting of representatives they stated their hope that the Birmingham would withdraw 'their intention of executing a Canal into Mr. Loxdales land or to Walsall as they imagine their proposed scheme will be more serviceable to the Miners'.[23] This was refused and plans approved for three extensions.

This was, of course, the time of the canal mania, and notice was given of no less than seven canals in the Birmingham area in four weeks of August and September 1792. As one local journalist put it: 'The Canal Bills so multiply, and the petitions for and against them so increase, that they promise to be as tedious as the trial of Mr. Hastings',[24] while one wag inserted an advertisement of a canal from Black Boy Yard, Birmingham to Carpenters Mill, Worcs; 'the Expence of cutting will be small ... from the purling Stream of the Pudding Brook running in a direct Line, which also renders it unnecessary to introduce *a single Lock or a single Yard of Tunnelling*'.[25]

The Birmingham company, however, were serious, and pressed on. Smeaton was asked to help by checking the plans and letters were written to reassure Loxdale and to deflect the opposition of the Staffs & Worcs Canal. The London committee set up to oppose the Selly Oak Bill dealt also with the new Bills. Opposition came from the Hon Mrs Edward Foley and Mrs Whitby, coheiresses of Thomas Hoo, who said that they wished to link their mines by canal to Walsall but that the new canal would prevent this by surrounding them so that the Birmingham company would 'monopolise the Conveyance of the whole of the Petitioners Canals at Bradley ... and thereby prevent [their] Mines from being carried to any other Market than along their Canal Navigation'. It was claimed that, to ensure this, the proposed canal terminated at an uninhabited place between Walsall and the mines.[26] Opposition from Edward Foley himself led to the withdrawal of the Soho section of the Bill and the Broadwaters section was not resubmitted separately that session, though construction began on the cut from the Broadwaters engine.

Before next session a line was discussed with the Staffs & Worcs Canal to run from Broadwaters to Monmoor Green, estimated to cost £20,425, but this appeared in the application to Parliament as a line from Broadwaters to Wolverhampton. A plan was also laid before the committee for a line through Coseley Hill from Bloomfield to Deepfield to eliminate the loop.

Local landowners led by Edward Foley put forward their own scheme for a canal from Broadwaters to Walsall. Since, as Houghton remarked, it was a 'puny scheme . . . if their Agents and Officers are to exist should think they must do more than consume the whole produce of the Canal',[27] it is not surprising that, at a meeting in January 1794, it was agreed that this should be built by the Birmingham Canal. The estimated costs of the proposed lines (which were embodied in two Bills for fear of the opposition to the third) were:

Broadwaters–Walsall	£35,943
Bloomfield–Deepfield	£19,210
Broadwaters–Wolverhampton	£20,493
	£75,686

and powers were sought to borrow another £85,000.

As anticipated, the opposition to the second Bill was strong and the third line was abandoned, the other two having an easy passage and receiving the Royal Assent on 17 April.[28] The Act changed the name of the company to Birmingham Canal Navigations and gave powers for the proposed lines and three collateral cuts (Broadwaters–Bradley, Darlaston–Bilston and Darlaston–Willenhall). The Walsall canal had to be completed within three years with maximum dues of 3d per ton for coal and 1½d for other goods, an extra 1d per ton on everything being allowed to pay the expenses of the subscribers to the rival Bill. Additional borrowing powers of £45,000 were granted to finance all this.

Work began immediately, the level cutting first, to be filled from Bilston Brook so that earth could be boated from the cutting to the James Green embankment, a 'navigable trough' being laid across the valley to link the cutting to the embankment. The Coseley line met objections from landowners and construction was suspended, except for a section to accommodate the Rev Cartwright's mines. A request for another 300yd to be cut to serve Beebee & Co's mine was turned down because of the shortage of funds, even though thirty boats a week were promised.

Money was indeed short; the proprietors were asked to find lenders at 5 per cent and in 1797 the dividend was cut because, although the money was available, the lack of lenders made it necessary to use it for construction. Nevertheless, and in spite of hitting a patch of running sand, it was hoped in October 1797 to open the Walsall Canal by the following midsummer if money could be found. It was only at this stage, even more late in the day than usual, that a contract was drawn up with the two contractors, Messrs Twigg and Smith, whereby they were to complete the canal by 1 January 1799, receiving 2s 2d (11p) per man/day and keeping 100–110 men constantly at work.

At this point Matthew Boulton requested that a cut be built across Birmingham Heath towards Soho, since he received his coal and sent his goods by land carriage to Birmingham wharf. After some to-ing and fro-ing with the Enclosure Commissioners for Birmingham Heath the extension, with a basin at the junction paid for by Boulton, was eventually completed early in 1801.

The Walsall canal proceeded without incident. It was opened to Loxdale's colliery on 11 December 1798 (having been held up for six weeks while a new turnpike road was completed) and throughout at the end of June 1799, 'on which occasion a boat load of coal was given by the Hon Mrs Foley and Mrs Whitby and distributed to the poor of the place'.[29] They presumably felt they had something to celebrate.

There remained the Bloomfield to Deepfield section. In August

1798 it had been agreed to continue cutting at a rate sufficient to supply the 'considerable quantities' of earth necessary to keep up the banks in areas of subsidence. Soon after Messrs Whitmore and Norton submitted designs of 'a forty foot Lock of a new construction'[30] to go at each end in place of the tunnel. One rather regrets it was not adopted; it would have added a new dimension to canal navigation. It was decided to use the small amount of money in hand after completing the Walsall canal to proceed with the tunnel, which was to be 16ft wide, 'about twelve men' to be employed on the work during the winter. In the spring the headings and shafts were advertised for letting and tenders accepted. However, Twigg, who had the contract for the cuttings, was promised 'such allowance for the advanced price of Wages in consequence of the high price of provisions as . . . shall appear right and proper' and this led to a decision at the beginning of 1801 that the section was 'not immediately necessary for public accommodation'.[31]

This was not the end of the improvements, however. Mine-owners were still insistent on their need for better accommodation, especially when opening new pits, and there was consequently a constant need to discuss new branches, some of considerable extent. Between 1801 and 1817 there were ten such applications, costing from a few hundred to several thousands of pounds. One may be cited to illustrate the problems.

In April 1802 Wilkinson asked for a half-mile extension to be built from the Walsall terminus to his limeworks. The cost was estimated at £2,000 and the cut rejected because it was felt it would not pay. In August 1806 he suggested he build it himself, but the committee requested time to consider the 'propriety' of doing it for him, and surveyed possible routes and cargoes once again. The expense was still £2,000 but it was hoped that the cut might provide extra water. The owners of quarries, mines and quays on the route were approached and agreed to 1½d per ton and all their water in return for 'free access to commodious Wharfs to be made at the termination of the proposed Cut',[32] but the committee were not happy with the proposed route and ordered a resurvey. Three more years elapsed and then, following a report that 8,930 tons were now got, which would rise to 11,800 when the canal was in use, the committee suggested 2d per ton provided that (as was suggested by the quarry owners) traffic reached 47,200 tons per annum. Since nothing more happened for another two years it is hardly surprising that a Mr Walhouse advertised his plan to build a railway instead, although he was prepared to give way to a canal. The quarry owners agreed to pay the 2d and the company agreed to go ahead 'upon the terms agreed upon in Novem^r 1810'. Rennie submitted a plan, but some mineowners objected because they were excluded from the route. The committee agreed 'that the proposed Cut be executed upon such plan as will render the Mine Owners the most extensive accommodation & that they are ready to carry it as far as desired ... if within the limits prescribed by the Act say (200 yards)'.[33] By this time the estimated cost had risen to £4,300 for the branch to Walhouse's land, plus another £5,300 for the additions. For some reason this had fallen to £2,802 within a week, which the committee felt could be built for 3d a ton. This was agreed, but legal opinion was taken as to whether the committee (as opposed to the proprietors) could make such a cut and whether the mineowners could bind their successors. The reply was that the committee could make it but that it must be free of toll. Not surprisingly it figures no more in the minutes!

At the same time the company was making improvements which it considered necessary in the existing line of canal. At the end of 1801 the committee were considering a shortening of the canal 'from Ladywood Lane Bridge to the Bridge at Birmingham Heath' (ie cutting off the Icknield Port Loop), which was estimated to save 979yd and cost £3,330. The matter remained in abeyance, however, and eventually, after a shorter embankment had been rejected, costing £1,070.50, a short cut was made to improve the corner at 'Sandy turn' at the Birmingham end of the loop. It was completed at the beginning of 1806 and a year later the committee, on one of their periodical tours of the canal, decided that 'a more extensive improvement here is worthy the

Committees attention—viz to make a Cut in a strait line from Bridge to Bridge which would improve the Navigation and leave as much of the present Canal as may appear necessary to contain Boats out of employ & eligible situations for Dockyards which have been found annoyances upon the line of navigation'.[34] Two more years elapsed and the committee decided that the proper line for the necessary embankment would be straight rather than on a curve, but the matter then disappeared from view until 1816, when an estimate was made of £1,164 and eight advantages listed, which included, '5th, To prevent Rail Roads or other Canals' and '6th, To employ the poor at the present time—better than a subscription of £500 which may be expected'.[35] The latter suggests some urgency, but, although it was agreed to go ahead, the line was finally built only as part of the much greater changes made by Telford.

Many minor changes were of course being made all the time, such as the provision of stabling at Farmer's Bridge to prevent the boatmen starting late in the morning from the need to fetch their horses long distances (which cost £240) or the widening of towpaths (£413). The constantly increasing traffic, 'which the opening of the Grand Junction may further increase', led to a decision to apply to Parliament for increased powers. The Bill had a relatively smooth passage, opposed only in one section by the Staffs & Worcs Canal who claimed that a reduction of tolls on small coals for steam engines would benefit the Worcester & Birmingham Canal, who would be under the necessity of raising water from the Severn. It became law on 3 July 1806[36] and permitted the company to make any improvements which became necessary without recourse to Parliament and without suffering a reduction of tolls even if the length of the canal were reduced—provided they fixed 'Posts or other Marks, dividing such shortened Line into a Number of proportionate Spaces corresponding to the Miles . . . on the original Line'. Power was granted to raise £100,000 in annuities to pay off existing mortgages.

The next year Rennie was employed to survey the whole canal and suggest inprovements. His report was submitted to Watt and

Galton, who concluded that the best solution to the water problem would be a canal from the Walsall Canal to Salford Bridge, but could not be certain that it would be an economic proposition. A survey apparently proved hopeful, for it was decided to ask landowners on the route for support and some horse-trading ensued with the Grand Junction Canal to get their support. Five possible lines were discussed; that adopted was close to that finally built, thirty years later, as the Tame Valley Canal. Negotiations with interested parties (including the Warwick & Birmingham Canal, who wanted a communication from the upper level of the new canal to the Digbeth pond to save the need for pumping water back) continued throughout 1810 and a Bill was introduced in the next session. However, it met with the united opposition of all the local canals, the millowners and many landowners and the section concerning the new canal was withdrawn, leaving only an Act to regularise the existing Acts,[37] and, in particular, to allow the 500 existing shares to be divided into 1,000.

All this refers only to relatively major operations. All the time towpaths were being cleared and doubled, sections dredged, embankments strengthened and buildings erected—and not without problems of other sorts. 'Lamps Barrows & other Materials' were taken by contractors and used for other people's purposes. On one occasion this led to an 'Affray . . . in reclaiming Two of the Cos Barrows in use at foundation sinking near Hockley Turnpike by a Person to whom they had been lent by Chambers a Lockkeeper'.[38] Banks kept slipping and needed piling, and a successful experiment was made under Rennie's direction at using flat slopes to the banks instead. Brick arch bridges were substituted 'at a very heavy expence . . . for Swivel & Draw Bridges which have been found very prejudicial to the Navigation',[39] and iron rollers were placed on bridges to prevent wear from ropes.

The most controversial small improvement at this period, however, was without doubt the removal of the 'bar' between the BCN and the Worcester & Birmingham Canal. It was first mentioned as a possibility in 1803 when the committee ordered Houghton to investigate what Parliamentary powers would be necessary to preserve water 'in case it may become necessary to open a communication', though an official approach from the Worcester Canal did not come until two years later. They were told that the BCN wanted full security against loss of water, a prohibition of coals passing into the BCN or a satisfactory toll, a guarantee against any loss on the compensation tolls paid by the Warwick & Birmingham Canal and a similar guarantee against loss of tonnage on goods passing to and from the Staffs & Worcs Canal. Several meetings ensued with the Worcester, Dudley and Stratford companies, later joined by the Warwick & Birmingham. It was agreed that the BCN should apply for the Bill, which should allow them 1s 4½d (7p) per ton on all goods passing into their canal and a toll on all goods going via the Worcester and Stratford Canals to and from the Warwick Canal at Kingswood Junction, the Worcester Canal to get 1s 4½d per ton back on all coal entering the BCN and unloaded in Birmingham.

The petition for the Bill stated that the BCN was the only source of coal for the Worcester Canal since 'this year, and for several years last past, since the making of the Dudley Canal, the navigation of the said Canal hath been obstructed and rendered impassable, by means of defects'.[40] It was opposed by 'several Merchants, Manufacturers and principal Inhabitants' of Birmingham who claimed that, since it would open up new markets for coal, it would make it dearer in the town, 'a consequence likely to be attended with the most alarming consequence to the Manufacturers thereof'.[41] On 27 June 1806 the Bill, which had been opposed in Parliament by the Dudley Canal, fell by 57 votes to 33.

Two years later the matter was reconsidered as a result of Rennie's survey and report, the main fear still being loss of water via the Worcester & Birmingham Canal to the Stratford and the Warwick & Birmingham; it was felt that 'something less than 1s 4½d (7p) per ton 'would be adequate compensation for coals. It was decided to meet the Worcester and discuss the matter.' Meetings with them and Dudley company continued throughout

1808 and 1809 until at a meeting in January 1810, 'Mr. Shirley in the Chair who on the part of Lord Dudley & the . . . Dudley Canal declaring that no restraint upon Coals passing out the Worcester Canal . . . would be allowed no progress was made towards the removal of the Bar'.[42]

Some months later the Worcester & Birmingham tried again, offering to supply the necessary water to take boats which passed the bar into the Stratford Canal. In reply the BCN asked for a toll of 6d (2½p) per ton on coal coming in and everything going out (which represented a complete change of policy), the coal coming in to pay an extra 8d if it passed a lock; they were offered 6d, 4d and 6d. After more discussions, and a threat by the Worcester Canal to apply for the Bill alone, they offered the tolls asked, but the two companies to share the outward tolls (on coal only) equally. This was refused and things lapsed for a little longer, though the Worcester Canal began to keep an exact account of water entering and leaving.

By 1814 the Worcester & Birmingham was nearly complete to the Severn and they began to worry about water sources. Several letters were sent to the BCN, all of which met with evasive replies which the Worcester Canal construed as 'an indirect refusal to enter into any treaty upon the subject'. They were told that the BCN would talk water, 'the preliminary terms upon which communication with the two Canals may be effected being agreed upon' first,[43] and thereafter their need for water was unashamedly used as a means of forcing them to a suitable agreement. When a deputation from the Worcester Canal finally went to register agreement the BCN committee were 'of opinion that this Company may be able to furnish the Worcester & Birmingham Canal with a considerable quantity of Water'[44]—though terms had to be agreed. In spite of problems about payment for water the Bill was read a first time on 9 February 1815, but strenuously opposed, there being a public meeting in Wolverhampton which decided unanimously that the compensation arrangements would be 'unequal in their effect & highly unjust & injurous to the Public'[45] and a meeting of local canals, all of whom raised some objections.

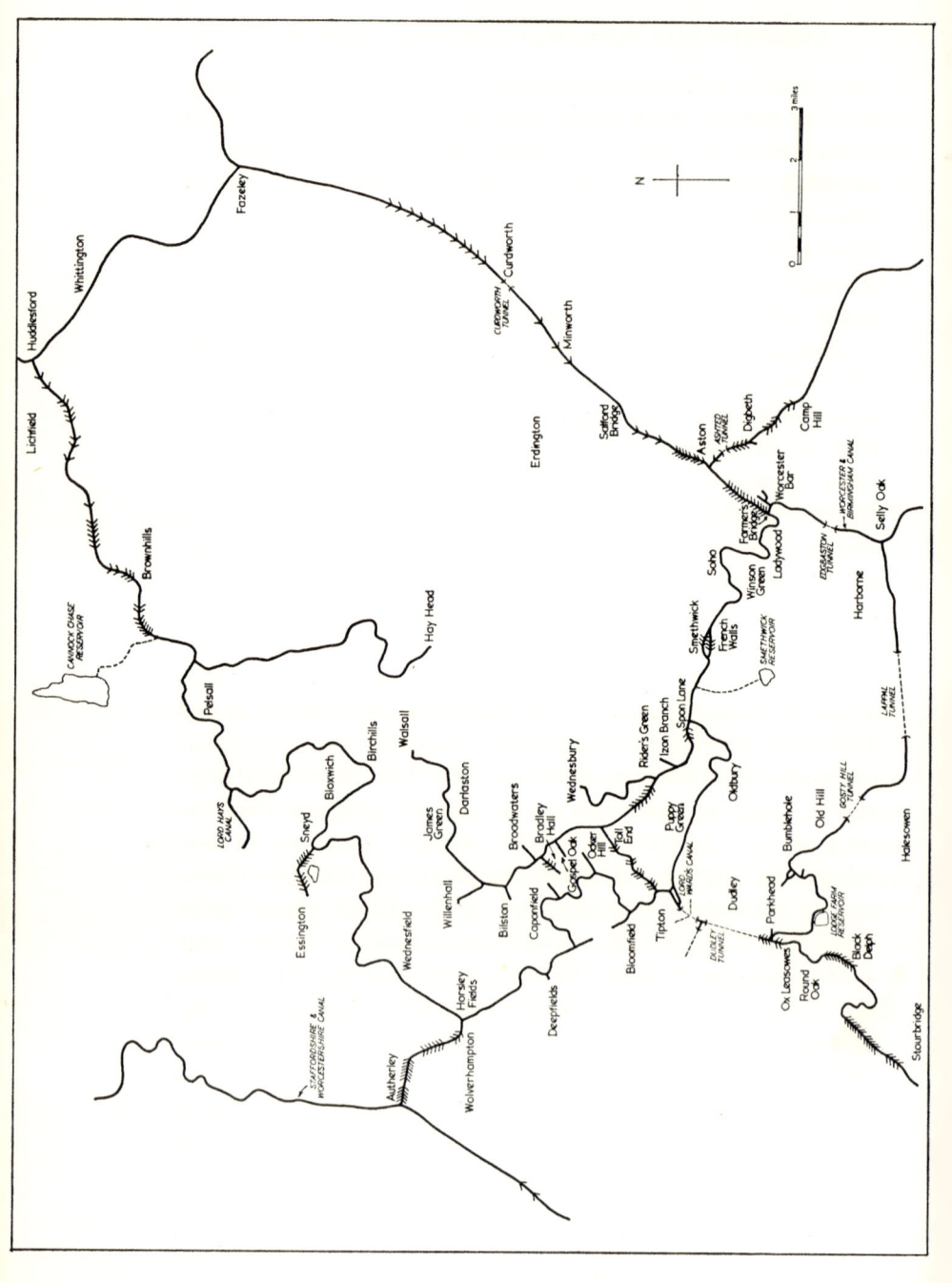

IMPROVING THE BIRMINGHAM CANAL, 1778–1818

The BCN had to yield and opposition was withdrawn upon agreement to 4d per ton on all goods going through the bar lock, with 4d more if they went through Farmer's Bridge locks and 2d more if unloaded at the BCN wharfs. The Royal Assent was given on 12 May 1815.[46]

Apart from the agreed tolls the main concern of the Act was with water, which was to be paid for at the rate of 3s per 4,000cuft whenever it stood more than 6in higher in one canal. The construction of the lock was described as for that on the Dudley Canal and it was to be shut 'at all . . . Times when the Darkness of the Night may render the Passage of Boats dangerous, or the Loss of Water to either Canal may be thereby in hazard'.

There then ensued a long wrangle about water supply, the Worcester Canal asking for 300 locksful each week and the BCN worrying about how it should be measured. In the meantime an emergency demand for water was met by extra working of the engines at Caponfield and Ocker Hill; a regular supply was withheld until this had been paid for (£185), together with a share of the cost of the Act (£595)—and this was not until May 1816. Discussions then ensued as to the price, the BCN asking 4s per lockful, the Worcester Canal offering 3s, but agreeing 4s provided it was available at three days' notice. The Worcester Canal suggested it could be measured by a lock so designed that the paddles at each end could not be raised together or by the calculation of the rate of flow through an aperture but finally agreed to take the superficial area of the Birmingham Level multiplied by the depth drawn off (thus presumably paying also for lockage water at Farmer's Bridge and Rider's Green!) Even so, as late as 1820 the Worcester Canal were in dire straits and having to be reassured by Houghton to prevent them seeking 'a certain and infallible supply' elsewhere.

CHAPTER 5

Telford and After, 1818–47

IN 1818, as the financial situation cleared, the Birmingham Canal recommenced its development. In May coalowners were informed 'that the Committee are desirous to improve the Line of the Canal from the Collieries to Birmingham', especially Bloomfield–Deepfield, the Brades–Oldbury Brook, Smethwick–Winson Green, and at Rotton Park, Botany Bay and Sandy Turn. It was decided to lengthen the planned tunnel at Coseley to save expense and to purchase mines beneath it. Then, at the end of the year, a sub-committee was appointed 'to make inquiries into the advantages and disadvantages & the propriety or impropriety of proceeding in the execution of all or any' of the proposed improvements. As a result it was decided to buy the land for Coseley tunnel but not to proceed further because of its 'too great magnitude & uncertain expediency', to start on Oldbury–Brades and to prepare plans for Winson Green–French Walls and for Rotton Park–Sandy Turn.

Wider issues were raised at the beginning of the next year when a Mr Price was interviewed by the committee about his proposal for a new cut to link Riders Green with the Toll End Communication to open new coalfields—what later became known as the 'Island Line'. It was agreed in principle but slept for three years. At the same period it was decided not to make a junction with the Wryley & Essington Canal at Walsall because lockage would make it an uneconomical route.

In May 1820 the Oldbury–Brades cutting was let in two lots for £459 and £1,450, and other deviations were brought under consideration. However hard rock was struck at the Brades and the first contract had to be raised to £1,071. It was filled with water in May 1821, the committee being very pleased, 'and they trust that in this as in other facilities ... the Proprietors ... will not only find stability but that increase of their Revenue will keep pace with public accommodation'.[1] The number of boats for Birmingham ticketed at Tivedale office rose as a result from 5,133 annually to 7,056. Next year the plan was approved for an improved line between Ladywood and Deep Cutting at a cost of £3,391 and for a deviation between Owens Lane and Tipton Factory, 'where the turns in the Canal are very acute & where ... meeting Boats frequently obstruct one another and collect in great numbers.'[2]

At this stage Mr Price revived his request for a new line from the old Wednesbury branch to Tipton and a preliminary survey was made of a route 8¾ miles long estimated to cost £4,750 exclusive of land. A few months later an even bigger change was contemplated, the engineer being asked for an estimate for 'opening a level communication between the Birmingham Pond and the old Wednesbury Branch'[3] bearing in mind consequent savings on wear and tear of Smethwick locks and the use of Smethwick and Ocker Hill engines. By this time, however, it had been decided that it was 'desirable that Mr. Telford should be engaged to examine the whole of the Line ... with the view of reporting generally such measures as may appear to Him to be expedient for improving the same'. He accepted on 2 April 1824, 'with much satisfaction' and paid his first visit on 28 June.[4]

He toured the canal for four days with Houghton, Freeth and the two engineers and has recorded his first impressions:

> I found adjacent to this great and flourishing town a canal little better than a crooked ditch, with scarcely the appearance of a haling-path, the horses frequently sliding and staggering in the water, the haling-lines sweeping the gravel into the canal and the entanglement at the meeting of boats incessant; while at the locks at each end of the short summit crowds of boatmen were always quarrelling ... and the mineowners, injured by the delay, were loud in their just complaints.[5]

Within two months he had ensured a new towing path at Ladywood and his overall opinion was that it was 'absolutely necessary that the numerous bends should be cut off, and the canal reduced to nearly a direct line from the town to Smethwick', with a new cut through the summit and 'the strait line . . . continued across the flat ground, called the Island, and the ridge at Bloomfield'.[6] He also proposed widening the canal to 40ft with walled banks and towpaths on each side. Most of these improvements, apart from the Island Line, were agreed by the committee in September, at an estimated cost of £27,520, of which £19,209 was the net cost of lowering the summit. The Island Line was suggested by Freeth at the end of September and surveyed soon after.

Telford advised that plans should be drawn up with longitudinal sections every 50 to 100yd and promised proper specifications by the end of October. However, 'important national business' delayed him until 20 December when he made a new survey which was reported on Christmas Eve, including several improvements added 'upon mature consideration'. These mainly concerned increasing the dimensions of the old summit both in width and depth and varying the line across the Island, including two branches, and would cost £15,500. He promised plans and sections by 6 January, 'leaving 20 Days for the Contractors to examine the said Documents and make their Estimates'. (The plans were not sent until a month later when he wrote, 'on his way to Ireland', suggesting three possible contractors who must be allowed four days to look at them). The committee agreed and decided to borrow £20,000 at 4 per cent—in the first place by reissuing assignments for money borrowed under the Acts of 1783 and 1793. The soil was removed from the proposed improved line at Spon Lane in February.

However the General Assembly in March heard that proprietors 'well acquainted with the Ground at Smethwick' had persuaded Telford 'that the removal of so large a quantity of Earth, as would be required to connect upon the same level the Birmingham and the Old Wednesbury Pond could not in the present state of the Canal be accomplished in a reasonable time without very injurious interference with the Trade'[7] and it was agreed to postpone this for the present. Even so money was required urgently and it was decided soon after to sell the company's disposable property (including 28 shares), to borrow £10,000 and to apply for some money still available from the last Exchequer Loan for Public Works.

The mineowners were urging speed with the Island Line and the committee took advantage of this by a decision 'that the Owners of Mines . . . into whose Lands, any . . . Branches may be intended to pass, shall be required to enter into an engagement to deliver into the Canal, all water raised from their Mines . . . free of all charges or expense'.[8] The matter of lowering the summit in order to communicate with the Island direct was also raised with Telford 'with a view to determine the eligibility of their execution within such time and upon such reduced scale as he may consider adequate to the exigencies of our canal', while guarding against competing schemes that may otherwise arise'.[9]

The 'exigencies' were financial. Eighteen months had passed since Telford had given his estimates, many detailed changes of plan had been made, and yet no revised estimates appeared until March 1826 (see p 102). In February 1826, Galton, chairman of the Finance sub-committee was 'much concerned' that there were no means of ascertaining with precision the probable cost of the new works. He estimated that, in addition to £87,687 already spent, £96,500 would be needed. Only £61,655 had been raised, so there was already a deficit of £26,032, borrowed from the General Cash Account. He reported that the first loan of £50,000 from the Exchequer Loan Commissioners was under way and another £50,000 was to be asked for. However, a month later Freeth reported no reply to a request for £85,000, by which date the treasurers had advanced £3,000 and there were no funds to pay the dividend. It was decided that if the loan did not materialise it would 'become necessary . . . to suspend the Progress of the greater part of the New Works for want of a means to carry them on'.[10] A week later T. Eyre Lee, who was in charge of the negotiations for the loan, reported that the commissioners were unwilling to lend to the company since its credit was so good 'that any Persons would cheerfully lend them money', but had agreed to lend £38,000, to be repaid over eight years, 'but it is a great matter I assure you in the existing state of things to have got this done'. Telford estimated £84,806 was still required and it was decided to ask the General Assembly to go to Parliament for new borrowing powers, since the total available from all sources was only £40,000, and that some works must be suspended. The company was even reduced to giving commission to persons who could raise loans.

A problem arose about checking the contractors' work because Telford made contracts with them in a 'short way . . . all the minutiae of the prices forming the aggregate amount are detailed in a book Kept by Mr. Telford . . . by which he Kept a strict and methodical check . . . as to every yard of work done the prices for doing which are Known only to Mr. Telford and'[11] the contractor. At this stage, too, Telford and Watt suggested that the canal be walled, 'as a walled canal of 30ft wide affords more room for boats than a canal of 40ft wide with slopes which the boats cannot come near' and drew attention to the need for water now Caponfield had gone. Telford considered 'the former mode of obtaining water . . . A vexatious source of perpetual conflict' and suggested reservoirs which were given priority in the time of scarce funds.[12]

Apart from the reservoir, which was at Rotton Park, eventually covering 80 acres, and 46ft deep, supplied by feeders from Oldbury 'across ridges and dingles, in such manner as to intercept the flood-waters of the upper country', all other improvements were interlinked. Nevertheless expenses had greatly exceeded estimates. It was therefore decided to continue all the works but to slow them down in such a way as to bring them all into operation at the same time; 'by reason of their uniting with the Old Lines at . . . Right Angles, the use that could be made of any One of them separately would be inconsiderable (without incurring much expence in easing the turns)'.[13] Telford was asked for two estimates for lowering the summit, one to be the cheapest way, 'independently of Ulterior Improvements in the Island', the other to be with the spoil made available from those improvements. Telford reported that 'neither Oeconomy nor Expedition' would be gained from separating the cutting down of the summit from the embankment across the Island and defended his extra expenditure because 'the Improvements are proportionately more extensive and perfect', and 'not beyond what the [public] had a just Claim for'. 'In his Opinion, the Reduction of the Summit Level was the most effective Step that could be taken, to render any Attempt to carry Mineral Products to Birmingham by a Railway, completely futile and unavailing'.[14] In August land was bought for the summit and the Island, and by October the first stage of the new reservoir at Rotton Park merely awaited rain to fill it.

Meanwhile money continued a problem. A sub-committee of three was set up 'to examine the state of the Finances of the Company in reference to the New Works' and a case was submitted to counsel to determine the company's borrowing powers; two said borrowing was lawful but two disagreed. Three others then said it would be lawful to pay the contractor in debentures for due consideration—the completion of authorised work—but this means was not used, the company continuing to borrow on debentures from the public at the 'high rate of Interest of 5 per Cent', on the basis that they could not see 'what difference it can possibly make whether a Debenture be issued to the Contractor ... or to Parties who lend the Money with which the Contractor is paid'.[15] Be that as it may, the result was satisfactory and the problem did not arise again until the new works were nearing completion and the company wished to redeem the debt with new debentures at a more favourable rate. It was as well this source was found, for costs were exceeding estimates at a surprising rate. In November 1826 it was reported that £48,278 was needed to complete works in progress and £125,743 for the summit and the Island, in addition to £192,056 already spent, of which £135,967 had been borrowed (£8,340 had been raised by selling 24 shares, the equivalent of £2,780 for each original £140 share!)

Negotiations with Mr Levy, a stock broker, for the loan of £100,000 had to be broken off when he insisted on negotiable bearer bonds.

It was now (January 1827) decided to apply all resources to lowering the summit to provide 'a free vent . . . for the Mines on the Old Wednesbury and lower Levels, and [free] the Coal Trade of the Canal, . . . from its present shackles'. However Telford reported that the 'space enclosed by the Embankment at Rotten Park may with advantage, and at a comparatively modest expense, be connected into a Reservoir to receive occasional flood Water';[16] it was surveyed, landowners approached and the go ahead given.

The new line to Smethwick was officially opened on 3 September 1827, the committee traversing it in the company's boat; 'the carriers and traders who attended expressed in the most decided and unequivocal terms their strong sense of the important advantages and facilities afforded by the new line and particularly by the double towing path'.[17] By this time the excavation at the summit was already 'very considerable, many teams and horse-runs and a great number of men [being] actively employed',[18] but the Island Line was still not started, though the mines in the area were being rapidly taken up and blast furnaces were being erected, promising profitable trade for the future. The plans were drawn up in December and an estimate accepted of £9,060, about twice that originally made, but they were not finalised for another year, by which time the contracted price was £10,935.

A new and expensive branch to Ridgeacre had been opened in September and an estimate of £7,135 was now accepted for the Bentley branch, merely two of the more important of the many relatively minor extensions which were constantly being approved while the major works continued. The original contract date for the summit cutting was midsummer 1830 but the contractor agreed to speed up the work in return for £500 for every month saved. A communication between the new line and the Birmingham pound, along which spoil could be boated, was made in May 1828 and a new cut from Tipton fourth lock pound to the Dixon branch, eventually to be part of the Island Line, was opened in the same month. As there was not time before winter to erect a cast-iron aqueduct to carry the old main line over the new cutting at Spon Lane it was decided to erect a two-arch brick aqueduct instead which was named after Steward, a prominent member of the committee. Meanwhile the connection between Bloomfield and Deepfield, so long delayed, went on apace.

New stop and gauging locks were planned on the New Summit Line at Smethwick 'for the protection of the Company's revenue', and new regulations for maintenance drawn up with the approval of Telford. The preamble stated that, in view of the 'great and incessant trade . . . and the breaches and sinkings hourly taking place . . . the first thing to be done is to establish a system of active and regular superintendence',[19] to which end three walking inspectors were to be appointed for each of three districts, to record maintenance needs and take immediate action.

Then, just as the major work, at the cutting, was nearing completion, in November 1829, an earth slip occurred bringing down 16,000 cu yd of earth, 'occasioned by the lodgement of water, at the back of the slope, between strata of silt and gravel'. This had to be drained by a tunnel. It was hoped it would be repaired within three weeks but was found worse than had been thought; the towpath walls had to be piled and more water kept coming from the tunnel as work proceeded. It was not until 18 December 1829 that Telford could report the new line ready for opening (and even then the tunnel was not completed); upon receipt of the news the committee 'resolved that this Committee do proceed forthwith in their Boat to open the New Line'. It must have been a notable sight; even today, to eyes accustomed to the works of railways and motorways it is impressive:

> The greatest depth of cutting is seventy-one feet; the waterway . . . is made forty feet wide, and five feet six inches deep; it is walled with stone on each side; and [has] a towing-path, twelve feet wide on each bank . . . At the place of greatest excavation is erected the largest canal bridge in the world; it is made of iron: the arch is one hundred and fifty feet span, and over it passes a public roadway twenty six feet wide.[20]

This bridge, named after Samuel Tertius Galton, still (1972) carries the modern traffic of the region.

At the same time, though less impressively, water was let into the Island Line near Tivedale, stop planks being first prepared in case of accident to the embankment. The new line was divided into as many sections as the old had miles.

At the end of February 1830 Telford gave in his estimate of £9,949 for the Anson branch. Townshend, the contractor for the summit, tendered for £10,385 and refused to reduce his offer until pressure was brought to bear, finally accepting Telford's figure. Telford reported work 'proceeding in a regular manner' on the Island, Gower branch and feeder, and it was agreed to extend Haines branch for the benefit of Horace St Paul, but the tempo was clearly slowing down. Puppy Green aqueduct, which was only partially complete, was suffering damage as a result but a decision as to its completion was deferred.

Renewed complaints therefore ensued from the mineowners about the Island Line and in October it was agreed to complete as far as the new mines at an estimated cost of £2,250, and to continue the Gower branch to a junction with the old canal (cost £6,435), thus enabling them 'to postpone executing the remaining part of the Island Line until the Landowners petition[ed]' for it to be done. It was decided that a junction between the Gower branch and the fourth lock pound at Tipton 'would produce many of the advantages contemplated by the original Island line', but the final decision, at one-sixth the cost, was to continue it to a junction with the existing canal at the Brades, by three locks, the top two being a staircase—though these were not completed until 1835.

At about the same time the cuttings at Bloomfield and Deepfield reached the points where tunnelling would need to begin and work was stopped. It was not until another year had passed that the mines under the intended tunnel were purchased. In December 1831 it was decided 'it is not expedient to continue the present expensive Engineering Establishment which it was deemed necessary to adopt during the progress of the New Works which have now been completed' and the resident engineer

(McKenzie) was given notice from midsummer 1832, the committee announcing that they had 'no intention at present of making any appointment of Engineer'.[21]

This did not prevent continued pressure for completion of the planned works, but this was resisted. Ironmasters requesting more work on the Island Line in April 1832, for example, were told that 'whilst this Company are desirous at all times to receive any suggestions whereby the Trade of the Mining district may be accomodated . . . they regret that the heavy expenditure already incurred . . . will of necessity prevent them from undertaking it at present',[22] and this continued to be the committee's attitude until well into 1834. In April of that year, however, news came of a threat from the mineowners to promote a railway from Wolverhampton to Birmingham if Coseley tunnel were not soon completed and this forced the Birmingham committee to order a report, as a result of which matters began to move:

> The circuitousness of the present line, between Bloomfield and Deepfield, and the want of better communication between the several levels, but more especially between the Wolverhampton level and the Birmingham level, have long been complained of; and as respects the latter, it need only be stated, that a Boat in passing the two communications now existing between the Wolverhampton level and the Birmingham level, must in one instance descend 8 and ascend 12 locks [to the Walsall level and up]; and in the other, to avoid the passage of 17 Locks, go above 4 Miles round [to Spon Lane].[23]

Remedial action was begun and, following three requests, the ground was inspected for a new branch up the Titford valley, and to ascertain the practicality of a new line from Wolverhampton to the district on the other side of the Sedgely ridge, to which it was believed the 'Ten Yard' coal extended.[24]

At the same time preparations began for a new Bill which was originally merely to empower the company to mortgage tolls in order to pay off all debts and to empower the construction of several new branches as well as sundry lesser matters. When public notice of the Bill was finally given, however, it was far more radical, since it planned to 'consolidate, extend, amend and render more effective' the powers given under all previous Acts, as well as permitting construction of seven new cuts, including the Titford branch, a cut from the Gower branch to Puppy Green Lane, Tipton, and another from the Three Furnace branch to Soap Factory bridge, Tipton, these latter two completing the Island Line, and the completion of the Coseley tunnel.

Deputations were received from the Dudley and Warwick & Birmingham Canals, the former 'anxious to be on friendly terms' and offering assistance, at a price, and the latter wanting 'most favoured nation' treatment regarding any reduction of tolls. The Dudley Canal gained agreement to modify the water level at the Tipton stop-lock and to end their obligation to pay the lock-keeper and provide his house; they were put on the same basis as the Worcester Canal at the Bar lock. Compensation tolls were reduced to a maximum of 3d per ton for all goods using the tunnel in either direction and not travelling more than 2 miles on the Birmingham Canal. Concessions to the Warwick Canal included the substitution of an overall charge of 10d per ton on ironstone between Birmingham and Fazeley for the old rate of 1½d per ton/mile, at an estimated cost of £400 and an agreement (not in the Act) to balance any cut in the Bar Toll by a cut of half the size in the compensation tolls payable for goods entering the Warwick Canal. With these, and some other trivial concessions, the Bill became law on 17 June 1835.[25]

Work began soon after. A tender of £14,472 was accepted for Coseley tunnel, land was bought for the Titford branch, which was planned 30ft wide and 5ft deep, the Island Line was offered for tender in two sections and a commencement was made at deepening the Wolverhampton Level to 6ft. At the same time a new line was being considered from the Walsall to the Wolverhampton levels and it was decided to apply to Parliament 'with a view to prevent the interference and obstruction which may hereafter arise from the projects of Railway . . . Companies, if the making of such communication be long delayed', but it soon appeared 'inexpedient to proceed' and the project dropped.[26]

The Coseley tunnel did not proceed as fast as had been hoped, notwithstanding the gangs working three eight-hour shifts round the clock. The strata were jumbled by coal workings and one shaft which collapsed in January 1837 was not open and working again until August. Nevertheless, by November the cashier could refer to both the tunnel and to Titford branch as 'recently effected' and the Island Line as 'near completion'. It was opened on 2 April 1838.

The improvements were an immediate success in speeding trade and relieving the locks at Smethwick which were 'enabled, in consequence, to afford full accomodation to the Coal Trade from Rowley and Oldbury & from the New and extensive district in the Titford Valley'.

> It was commonly said at Birmingham, in consequence of this improvement that Mr. Telford ought to have had a public reward for introducing good manners among boatmen, who formerly seldom passed without quarrels and imprecations, arising from the difficulty and delay of passing the towing line below the inner boat; whereas they now meet and pass in good humour and with mutual salutations.[27]

The New Line even kept open throughout a severe winter and visitors came to admire it from the Mersey & Irwell Navigation and the Rochdale, Peak Forest, Macclesfield and Ashton-under-Lyne Canals. The company congratulated itself that

> The aggregate Business transacted on the various Lines & Levels of the Canal [aggregating eighty miles], exceeds probably, that transacted on any other Canal of equal extent ... With exception of that part of the Canal between Farmers Bridge and Digbeth, on no other Canal in the Kingdom, is the thoroughfare Trade conducted, with greater regularity and despatch.[28]

All was not, of course, for the best in this wonderful world. For one thing the expansion of industry along the canal was not an unmixed blessing. The 'stench and offensiveness of the filth' dredged from the canal in the town was particularly noticeable and there was nowhere to deposit it:

110   THE BIRMINGHAM CANAL NAVIGATIONS

FIGURE 3. Advertisement for one of the many factories established along the line of the canal

The great increase of Wharfs and Works in & near the Town, has not only rendered the mudding of the Canal more frequent, but by causing the adjoining lands to be so closely occupied by buildings has added greatly to the difficulty of doing the necessary work. Scarcely any convenience for a temporary depositing of mud in case of emergency is now to be found on any land adjoining that portion of the Canal which passes through the Town.[29]

The main problem, however, as mentioned above, was the locks at Farmer's Bridge. They were 'quite inadequate' for the increased trade, so much so that attempts were even made to re-route traffic via Worcester Bar and Kingswood to relieve them and a plan was made, but shelved, for a tunnel from the Hospital pound to Saturday bridge to connect with another recirculatory engine in an attempt to relieve the water problem. The locks were open day and night and Sundays but twenty or more boats were often queuing at each end. But no solution could be found unless the locks were by-passed. As early as 1830 it had been suggested that a parallel flight be built, but the land was so built up that the cost (£66,618) was prohibitive. Joseph Parkes therefore suggested a new cut from Worcester basin to Camp Hill on the Warwick & Birmingham Canal and the BCN agreed to co-operate provided each canal paid 'a proportion . . . equal to the actual advantage each company will derive from its completion'. When the Bill reached Parliament, however, it withdrew its support, merely paying £150 towards Parkes's expenses, and the Bill dropped. By 1839 there were 70 steam engines and 124 wharfs and works on the banks between Farmer's Bridge and Aston, and the cost of parallel locks had risen to £200,000. It was therefore decided to revive the 1810 plan for a canal from the Danks branch to Salford bridge, which would also pass through a district full of coal and 'would tend in a high degree to close the Valley of the Tame against future projects & by such Means, add greatly to the stability of this Concern'.[30] A special Assembly agreed on a draft Bill in December 1838, which later included also powers to reduce the bar tolls on goods leaving the Birmingham Canal.

The Dudley Canal of necessity opposed the Bill on the basis of the latter clause (they had, in fact, previously taken legal action to restrain the BCN from reducing tolls on outgoing coals only) and succeeded in getting the Bill recommitted to committee in order that their case be heard. The Birmingham Canal decided to withdraw the Bill rather than suffer a reduction in the inward toll, but had the problem that the Warwick and Stratford Canal would oppose if the outward reduction were removed. Finally the clause was removed entirely, the Birmingham Canal agreeing to cut the compensation toll on goods at Digbeth without an Act and to bring in another Bill the next session to cover the other tolls so that it could be amended if desired, 'the Delegates at the same time taking care not to pledge the Company to proceed with such Bill further than the Committee unless they should think proper to do so'.[31] The Act[32] received the Royal Assent at the end of June 1839.

Work on the Tame Valley Canal, as it was to be called, began soon after, notwithstanding the cashier absconding, leaving a deficit of £7,032. A member of the committee lent £25,000 and Messrs Walker and Burgess were appointed engineers. Their first report recommended considerable departures from the Parliamentary line, in particular to commence near Toll End on the Walsall Canal rather than from the Danks branch, to straighten the line, concentrating the locks at Perry Bar, and to link with the Daw End branch of the Wyrley & Essington Canal. This would require an embankment 40ft high for a mile, which was not large by the standards of new railway schemes though, as Walker put it, 'with the exception of your own great work, I am not aware of anything in Canals equal to the proposed embankment'. The estimated cost of the changes, which were agreed, was £50,000. A new Bill therefore became necessary and it was decided to include in it powers to build railways from the south west of Titford to the canal to serve new mineral districts. A request from the Warwick & Birmingham that a line be added from Salford bridge to Digbeth (the so-called Bordesley Canal, which had been first mooted in 1836) was rejected, the BCN later notifying its dissent when an independent Bill for this line was promoted (at this time called the Birmingham & Warwick Junction Canal).

Meanwhile James Walker suggested that the embankment be higher up the Tame valley, which would cut a third off the estimated cost and help the junction with the cut from Daw End. By some rather specious reassuring he showed that 'at the first there is no great difference of expense [from the Parliamentary line], and that in the long run, in this as in most other things, the best is also the cheapest',[33] and his plans were approved unanimously, a Mr Holland being appointed to supervise the construction of the new works. Work commenced on those parts not affected by the changes of the line.

However, great opposition was said to exist from the landowners on the route, which would require considerable expense to compensate, and the committee agreed early in 1840, again unanimously, to proceed with the Parliamentary line and drop the Bill. Walker was incensed, and said so in a very long letter to the committee. He suggested that their decision was caused by their having other concerns to distract them, since the facts were not as they stated; he had made slight changes which satisfied three of the four objectors and avoided the lands of the other, while the original line went via Newton Hill, 'the most expensive and troublesome part of the whole of the Grand Junction Railway'[34] as he had been informed by Mr Townshend, who built the section. The committee read his letter, considered it, and, again unanimously, reversed their decision.

The Bill therefore proceeded, parallel with that for the Birmingham & Warwick Junction, which the BCN opposed, though vainly, 'for the protection of the Water in that part of the Digbeth Pound as belongs to the Company'. The Tame Valley Bill passed the Commons intact but was opposed in the Lords by the Dudley and Stratford Canals who wanted the bar tolls equalised each way and who thus, so it was alleged, raised a constitutional issue since, had they been successful, the Lords would have altered a clause coming from the Commons relating to taxation of the subject. Be that as it may, a compromise was reached whereby the tolls remained as they were and the Bill became law on 4 June 1840.[35]

In August, Walker reported that the works were progressing well, the canal being built 30ft wide, walled part of its depth and with an 8ft towing-path on each side. He suggested that instead of connecting the Anson branch with the Wyrely & Essington by ten locks it should be continued only as far as it would go on the (Walsall) level, with another line on the same level from Wood Green to Portobello. This was agreed at the time but the line (the Bentley branch) was eventually built to the original plan.

In January 1841 fifteen tenders were received for the Tame Valley Canal ranging from £269,837 to £163,900 (£184,094 was accepted after one for £170,206 could not find sureties) and for the Bentley Canal, still without the ten locks, from £27,691 to

£11,300, the latter being accepted, Walker and Burgess being allowed 4 per cent of the cost. By now 'the pressure on the Locks at Farmer's Bridge . . . was excessive, but the impression that a new line is being provided being general, and the weather on the whole proving fine, the inconvenience was put up with without much complaint'.[36] During March 1841 4,877 boats passed the top lock, or 157 each day including Sundays. In June plans were approved for joining the Bentley branch first to the Wednesfield level (four locks) at an estimated extra cost of £6,850 and then to the Wyrley Canal. A tender of £19,208 for the whole was accepted from thirteen offers ranging up to £28,500. At the same time work commenced to bring the Wyrley Canal up to the standard of the Old Birmingham Canal, which was achieved by the end of the year.

No. 9.—TAME VALLEY CANAL.—JUNCTION WITH FAZELEY CANAL.

FIGURE 4. Salford Junction, c 1855

In April 1842 the committee had second thoughts about the Rushall branch, connecting the Tame Valley Canal with Daw End, and decided not to purchase the land necessary, even though it had to be done before April 1843 if their powers were not to lapse. Unfortunately, the solicitor informed them that the money borrowed under the Act of Union with the Wyrley Canal could, by that Act, be used only for the Bentley and Rushall Canals, and if the latter were not built, the remaining money (£60,000) would have to be returned. A decision was postponed and meanwhile

No. 11.—TAME VALLEY CANAL.—GIRDER AND BRICK BRIDGES.
NEWTON CUTTING.

FIGURE 5. Brick and girder bridges over the Tame Valley Canal near Perry Barr, c 1855

£300,000 was borrowed from the Bank of England, an indication of the company's standing. In June they decided to go ahead and buy the land.

In October 1842 John Merry reported on the new works on the Bentley branch which it was planned to open the next January:

> The Bridges have flat Iron plate tops, the Iron bearers resting on Brick pillars and are simple in their construction and appearance, every Bridge has an Iron rope rubber . . . and is furnished in the waterway with grooves for stop planks. The Locks are formed upon the plan of those erected at Walsall with chambers running along the sides and in consequence will be subject to damage in case of their sinking, they are coped with large blocks of Derbyshire Stone, and the Brick work of the entrances . . . is well protected from the striking of the boats, by strong Iron Fenders . . . there is only one paddle to each Chamber, which is raised by means of a windless and rack, the motion of which is so smooth that a boy of 12 or 14 years of age can work it, and as soon as the friction consequent on newness is reduced by use the rack will fall of itself after being wound up.[37]

It was at this point that Freeth, who had intended to retire on completion of fifty years service in 1839, but had been persuaded to stay on by a gratuity of £500 and a 50 per cent salary increase (from £500 to £750), decided that his ill-health forced him to resign. In his letters of resignation he claimed that he had taken over as clerk at a time 'particularly inauspicious as regards the Canal. The County was rife with rival projects, the Canal was totally inefficient . . . My first duty was to put the Canal in a state of safety'—which he did, so he alleged, by planning all those improvements usually attributed to Telford which were delayed by 'the idle fears of some and the mean jealousies of others'. Having done all this, and acquired the Wyrley Canal which might have become a rival, he 'considered [his] great task done, and . . . became anxious for some relaxation'.[38] He was given a pension of £375 but was later persuaded to stay on in a supervisory capacity for his pension plus another £225 per annum, Robert Thomas being appointed clerk.

In January 1843 a report put the cost of the new works—the Tame Valley, Walsall Junction, Rushall and Bentley canals together with Parliamentary costs—at £429,327, of which £321,278 was for the Tame Valley and £65,613 for 180 acres of land. The Bentley Canal was opened on 28 April 1843 (soon after which the Wood Green branch, which had been intended as a partial replacement for it on one level, was finally abandoned) and the Tame Valley on 14 February 1844.

Meanwhile it had been decided to apply to Parliament for new borrowing powers and to allocate the proceeds of the sale of land for the next three years to the Rushall Canal. The new act [39] became law uneventfully in April 1844. Plans for Rushall were approved in April 1844, 36ft wide with 9ft double towpaths, and it was completed in 1847. Owing to changes made in the tolls on the Coventry and Warwick Canals traffic on the Tame Valley Canal was never as high as had been hoped, but it was good. Between 600 and 800 boats used it each month, 'a portion [of which] may be considered in the light of a diverted trade, but many were of a character altogether new'.[40]

All this had not, of itself, solved the water problem. In July

1830 sixteen acres were bought to raise the 'outside margin of Rotten Park Lake' to 55ft above the Birmingham level and at the end of 1832 it was felt that this reservoir, together with the benefits from lowering the summit, meant that the company was 'in a considerable degree independent of the Mine Engine Waters now paid for'. It was decided to reduce the number of engines for which water payment was made and not to allow more to be used. A few months later it was decided to drain the Smethwick reservoir and let the land since it leaked so much, notwithstanding great expense in puddling, that little advantage had been gained from it for some years. In 1835 an engine was erected to pump surplus water from the Wolverhampton level into the Rotton Park reservoir and the dam was raised 3ft. A few months later another engine was installed 'that every possible advantage may be taken of the flushes that occur in rainy weather'. In September 1836 a new reservoir was being considered next to the existing one on the land bought six years previously, to be 5ft deep only, but the decision was rescinded in favour of one to widen the dam on the existing reservoir. The lockage on the Titford branch was met by a recirculatory engine and contributions were made towards mineowners' engines to drain mines into the Deepfield pond and to drain Caponfield from a lower level than before.

Nevertheless, in 1837 a dry season occurred during which the reservoir was exhausted 'earlier than usual . . . and for several Months the whole Trade of the Canal, was dependent on the supplies of water . . . afforded [by Mines Engines]—Many Engines were engaged expressly for the purpose . . . a heavy and unavoidable expence was the consequence'.[41] The merger with the Wyrley & Essington, however, brought with it the Cannock Chase reservoir. In November 1839 'the Company's Engines at Ocker Hill, Smethwick and Rotten Park [were] at a stand, the Water for the Lockage . . . being now wholly supplied from the Reservoirs and Mine Engines'.[42] By the next year water was being sold to neighbouring canals at between 5s (25p) and 7s 6d (37½p) per lock while 'the humiliating step of compelling Boats to wait turns at the Locks, was not resorted to at any one point throughout the

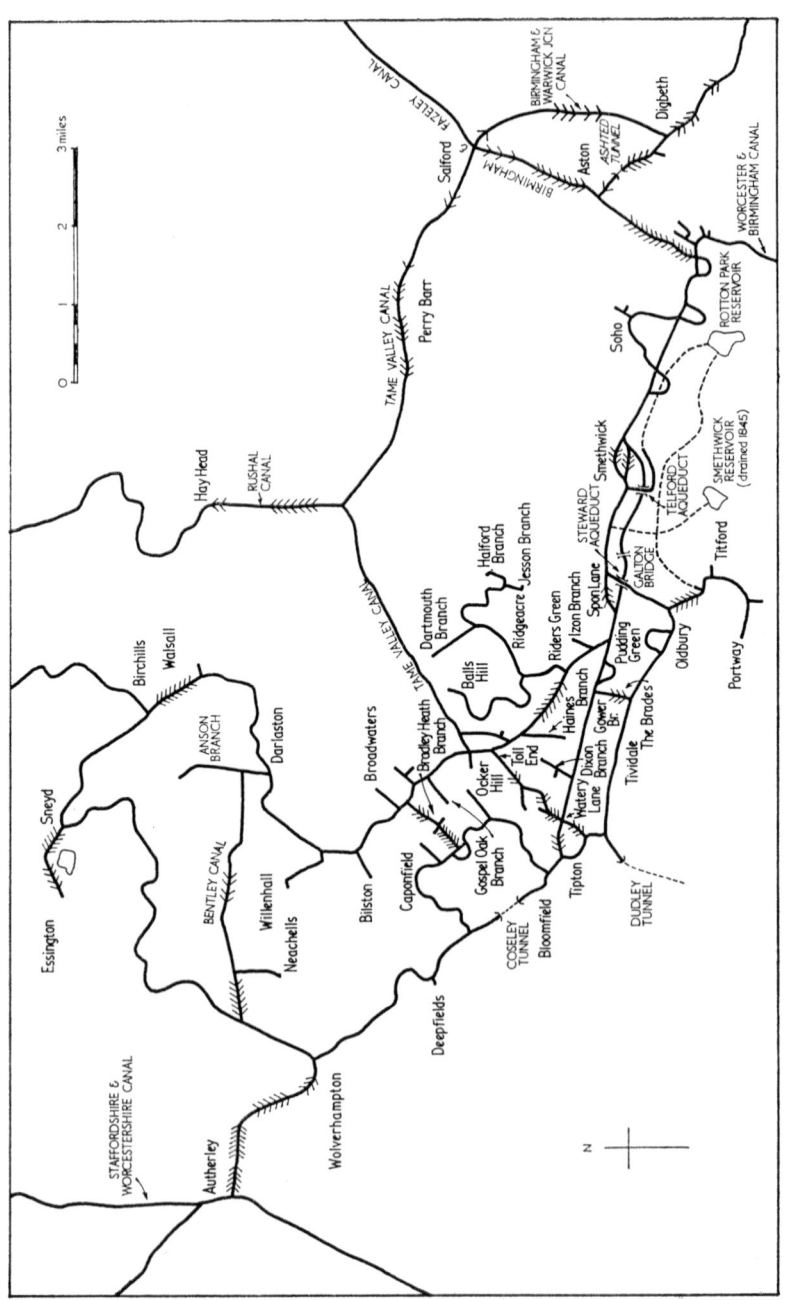

FIGURE 6. Map of developments, 1815–1847

whole of the extensive and complicated lines of the Company'. Even so 'the whole of the Water resources of this Company are barely sufficient in seasons of ordinary drought'.[43]

At the end, as at the beginning, it was impossible to maintain the traffic upon an extensive canal on a plateau in a mining area without constant attention to the problem of water. The Birmingham Canal was probably the most efficient in the country, but it had to be.

CHAPTER 6

Control and Finance

THE CONTROLLING GROUPS

As can be seen by a glance at the lists of proprietors, the canals of the Birmingham area were overwhelmingly locally financed; even places such as Wolverhampton were virtually unrepresented amongst the promoters of the original canal and this intense localism persisted throughout.

However, more important than the geographical location of the shareholders is the social and industrial background of the controlling group. In the case of the BCN, for example, the normal attendance at general assemblies varied between twenty-five and forty, with perhaps another twenty or thirty sending proxies—though the total of shares represented was usually around 400. From the lists of attenders and proxy-holders it can be seen that there were one or two groups of important size, usually controlling upwards of sixty votes and usually working amicably together. Since the Act forbade holdings of more than ten shares (later interpreted to mean other than those acquired by inheritance), the core of such groupings was usually a family, particularly the Galtons, the Lloyds and the Lees, who could usually command a majority if they acted together.

There were a few problems arising from this dominance, but they rarely became troublesome. Thus in 1830 James Taylor declined to be on the committee 'while there exists such an influence as last year was . . . employed in excluding him from it' and Samuel Tertius Galton complained of the 'serious inconvenience' caused by the solicitor to the company being the son of the chairman, himself one of the Lee family. The chairman had only just been restrained from filling a casual vacancy on the committee with his son's partner and the solicitor's family had collected proxies prior to Assemblies

> constituting together with their own votes, an overwhelming influence, amounting at different periods of the last ten years to one fifth, one fourth and even two sevenths of the whole number of votes of the General Assembly, independently of any votes or proxies held by the partner of the Solicitor.[1]

Galton's motion that a new solicitor be appointed was lost in committee, but the General Assembly decided in September of that year that no one using proxies at the General Assembly could be the solicitor.

However, few decisions required votes, once the Garbett/Colmore troubles were passed, and the committee was usually elected by agreement. It would therefore seem most useful to concentrate our attention on the members of the committee chosen by the controlling group to represent their interests.

Over the 78 years studied, only 98 persons served on the committee averaging nearly eleven years each; the 37 who served for ten years or more averaged 24 years each. Nearly all of these died in office. It is clear that these are the people who controlled the company, and it is upon them that analysis is concentrated. (See Table I, p 122).

They can be divided into four broad groups; landowners, professional men, merchants/manufacturers and those who called themselves merely 'gent'. The surprising thing, in such an area, is that of the dominant group of thirty-two only one falls into the first category; Lord Dartmouth was certainly a coalowner but he was clearly exceptional. He never attended a committee and was presumably retained for his Parliamentary influence. The professional men are also a small group, numbering only four though they provided the chairman for most of the period. The third group is the most interesting as well as the largest, providing twenty-three out of the total. Though it is difficult to subdivide with accuracy it seems about evenly divided between small manufacturers and merchants/bankers. None appear to be large users of coal; some at least would appear interested in importing and exporting over a wide area. The final group is more amorphous and apparently includes some from the third group who moved up in the world. Conflicts in the locality between coal-users and coal-owners seem never to have been reflected inside the committee, who seem to have viewed policies solely from the viewpoint of their effects upon the profits and prospects of the company.

This was probably a by-product of the Bentley/Garbett quarrel. Bentley and his group, all short-lived members of the committee, had the eighteenth-century attitude summed up in the word 'job'; a controlling position in a company was useful because of the possibility it gave of personal gain by using the company for one's private interests. People such as Ash, Lee and Galton, on the other hand, were modern-style 'company men' who saw their interests as being advanced with and through the company.

What we are investigating, therefore, is the behaviour of a relatively small, closely knit group, of similar public and private interests,[2] localised within a relatively small area centred on Birmingham, dominated, with no signs of strain, by a few large groupings through a committee whose members served long enough to develop a corporate sense. It is this which makes them so interesting as forerunners of modern corporations.

Table I
Committee Members of the BCN

Name	Years in office	Occupation and address
Ash, Dr John, M.D.	1770–94	Physician, Temple Row
Beaumont, Richard	1811–28	Gent, Ashted
Bayley, James	1829–37, 1839	Not known
Bingham, James	1796–1810	Bucklemaker, New Hall Walk

CONTROL AND FINANCE

Name	Years in office	Occupation and address
Boulton, Matthew	1768–9, 1802–9	Toymaker/engineer, Soho
Browne, Benjamin	1810–25	Not known
Browne, George, M.P.	1829–45	Gent (Son of Col. A. Browne, M.P.)
Dartmouth, Earl of	1770–1801	Landowner, politician
Francis, John	1771–87	Coffin-nail maker, Park Street
Freer, Rev Thomas Lane	1809–25	Rector of Handsworth
Galton, Samuel	1768–99	Gunmaker/merchant, Steelhouse Lane
Galton, Samuel, jnr	1777–83, 1787–1827	Merchant, Steelhouse Lane
Galton, Samuel Tertius	1815–43	Banker
Grice, Joseph	1807–28	Screwmaker, Handsworth Hall
Henn, Henry	1770–85	Merchant, Bull St
Hunt, Harry	1788–97	Gent, The Square
Hunt, William	1777–1808	Buttonmaker, Lichfield St
Kettle, John	1768–86	Steelmaker/Gent, New Street
Lane, John	1777–91	Grocer, Bull St
Lee, Thomas	1769–91	Attorney
Lee, Thomas jnr	1791–1840	Attorney
Lloyd, Sampson	1772–83, 1787–92, 1794–1807	Banker
May, Benjamin	1784–1809	Plater
Moilliet, J. L.	1834–43	Merchant/Banker
Pemberton, Samuel	1772–4, 1789–1803	Jeweller
Price, Rev Thomas	1786–96	Headmaster, Free Grammar School
Rabone, Richard	1772–83	Bucklemaker
Rolfe, William	1792–1803	Hardwood Turner, High Street
Russell, Thomas	1794–1825	Gent, New Street
Ryland, John	1780–1814	Wiredrawer, High St
Ryland, Samuel	1811–42	Gent
Scott, Robert	1832–45	Gunmaker, Stourbridge

Name	Years in office	Occupation and address
Steward, Col Samuel	1820–45	Gent
Taylor, James	1810–45	Buttonmaker, Moseley Hall (Worcs)
Watt, James, jnr	1804–45	Engineer, Soho
Wheelwright, William	1797–1828	Gent, Prospect Row
Wilkinson, Joseph	1768–80	Merchant, Snow Hill

The remaining 61 persons who served on the committee, averaging less than four years each, were divided as follows:

Landowners	1
Professional	9
Merchants etc	29
Gent	9
Not known	13

The Dudley Canal proprietors were different in several significant respects. They were certainly from the locality (with a few from Birmingham),[3] but they were few in numbers (only 22 in the early years) and the great majority called themselves 'Gent' or 'Esq', which means that they were probably landowners and therefore coalowners.[4] Throughout the dominating grouping was that of Lord Dudley and his family, though this appears to have been accepted by his fellow coal-owning proprietors.

After the Tunnel Act there was an almost complete change of control; only Lord Dudley and Richard Aston, another leading coalowner, remained from the old committee. However, the change was stable, thirteen persons, overwhelmingly coalowners, serving virtually unchanged on the fifteen-man committee until the Selly Oak period. Then several withdrew entirely from the company following disagreements; nevertheless nine of the new committee were coalowners and were joined by two ironmasters. Though Lord Dudley withdrew after the completion of the Selly Oak line his interest was clearly still respected and the company relied heavily upon his agents, Charles Roberts (d. 1811) and Francis Downing, the latter serving on the committee from

1822–43. Some Birmingham businessmen joined the committee after 1800, but the weight remained with coal and ironmasters until amalgamation.

This peculiarity of control, sharply distinct from that of the BCN, accounts for other distinguishing features. Only once before 1800 did the company pay a true dividend, and dividends were low thereafter. This would obviously tend to concentrate shares in the hands of those who had something to gain from using the canal even if this had not already been the case. In 1786 it was said of them:

> The Proprietors had only the coal trade in view, when they, who have considerable coal works ... undertook it ... the want of water limits the business, and in the Summer season very little trade can be carried on: But though it does not prove beneficial to the undertakers as Proprietors, yet they being the owners ... of coal mines have an ample advantage in the convenience of a Navigation to carry their property to market.[5]

We know much less about the committee of the Wyrley & Essington Canal since they did not give occupations in the lists of proprietors, as did the Dudley Canal, nor are there directories for this early period for the areas from which they were drawn. Rather surprisingly, considering the parallel nature of the route, there were links with the Staffs & Worcs Canal.

As far as can be ascertained, apart from James Hordern, a banker, who held eight original shares, Messrs Chrees and Wightwick, attorneys and later clerks to the company, who held six and eight respectively, and four clergymen (at least one of whom was a substantial coalowner), the original proprietors were all local manufacturers and gentry. This situation appears to have changed little during the life of the company, the committee, whose numbers tended to fluctuate, being, in general, stable as to its composition. Outstanding amongst the proprietors were the Vernons of Hilton Park, prominent local landowner/coalowners, two of whom held six original shares each while the Hon Caroline Vernon of London held six more.

We are probably justified in regarding this, too, as a coalowner's canal, though not in the extreme sense in which this description can be applied to the Dudley Canal. It is perhaps significant that their seal was a pit-head with a beam-engine.

FINANCE

When we turn to the detailed operation of the canals we are forced to deal mainly with the BCN since its documentation is so much more complete. There are, for example, no account books remaining for either of the other two canals before their merger.

The BCN kept very detailed accounts, but probably gained very little useful information from them. All monies received and spent were entered first in waste books and then transferred to the Journal. A ledger was kept, in full double entry, but it was used only to produce 'Balance Accounts', of which many volumes remain, checked by the auditors before each General Assembly. These are nothing more than vast records, in detail, of trial balances and, as such, provided a check on the accuracy of the clerks, but tell us (and the proprietors) little of any use about the prosperity of the concern.

As early as 1773 an *ad hoc* sub-committee was appointed to see whether accounts could be kept in a better manner, but with no apparent result. It was, however, agreed that the company should have a stock book and that all monies must be paid to and claimed from the treasurer. In fact all discussions about the accounts were of means to gain greater efficiency in recording (and, presumably, suppression of dishonesty) rather than in conveying information. Thus it was discovered in 1775 that account had been kept of goods arriving at Birmingham, as a check on toll receipts, but not on those leaving or on those being set down at intermediate points such as Spon Lane, and steps were taken to deal with this in future.

In 1813 a sub-committee was set up, consisting of Watt, Grice and Galton, to report on accounting procedures. Arising from this certain sub-committees were set up to supervise expenditures; one for fire-engines and water, one for accounts—'not merely to mark off the entries in the Cash Book & examine the arithmetical correctness' but 'to investigate the propriety of the expenditure of all Bills'—and one for 'the Cash Accounts of the Company & the liquidation of the Debt'.[6] The first minute of the Accounts Committee shows that the emphasis was still upon improved administration:

> The Committee ... are desirous at the commencement of their Undertaking to make a few preliminary observations an attention to which will not only lighten but give additional efficacy to their labour.[7]

These were to pay quickly to get good service, to pay within three months and ask for a discount and to keep a record of contracts and orders as made.

Besides supervising expenditures they recommended putting major items out to tender, in particular oak timber and scantlings, elm and deal boards and planks and iron castings. By 1818 the General Assembly could congratulate the committee

> for the Pains and Ability which they have taken in planning and promoting the financial Arrangements of this Company whereby in the course of a few Years they have been enabled nearly to discharge the heavy Load of Debt ... —a Measure which has been eminently instrumental in giving a Regularity to the Dividends of this valuable Concern and bringing it to its present State of Prosperity and Stability.[8]

Nevertheless, in 1821 the committee was still complaining of 'the system of extravagance which has for some years past been introduced' and adopted rules for the engineers which prevented them ordering materials, starting repairs or employing workmen without prior permission. Not surprisingly it became necessary to employ 'John Thomas a Carpenter to keep the Account of Materials received and delivered & in making out the Workmens & Labourers checks'[9] so that the system was not without its costs.

In 1820 the committee was empowered to invest a sum not more than 5 per cent of the dividend to accumulate for repairs and four years later, at the suggestion of Col Steward, a similar fund was set up for new works. It was given a separate column in the *Abstract of Accounts*, but still not separated from revenue expenditure.

Later, in 1827, another sub-committee was appointed to advise on a plan 'for regulating the money transactions of the Company' which recommended the use of cheques, to be signed by the clerk, for all payments of more than £10, including, where possible, dividends.

Throughout our period the general trend of dividends was upwards, as can be seen from the graph.[10] As far as can be seen, they were paid out of cash in hand, with no attempt to estimate true profits—though never so blatantly as by the neighbouring Staffs & Worcs Canal, who several times ordered, for example 'That the Treasurer . . . do make a Dividend of such Monies which shall then be in his Hands as he can conveniently divide upon the 27th Day of January next'.[11] Even so, there could be problems, as in 1845:

> Mr. Lloyd of the firm of Taylor and Lloyd bankers and treasurers of the Company said that sometimes gentlemen left the room after hearing the statements under the impression that the treasurers were deriving very large advantages from the balance in their hands . . . the balances set forth in the accounts did not represent actual amounts in the hands of the treasurers. Up to the night before [they] held only a balance £4,950-17-9 . . . the amount of the dividend alone would amount to £29,000 and he thought although it was necessary that a dividend be declared it would be advisable to fix another day for the payment of it.[12]

It was probably legitimate to concentrate on cash flow in days when this was often the limiting factor, but we are more interested today in the overall profitability of the concern. The accounts of the company were put into some order in the *Abstracts of Accounts* and the *Receipts and Expenditure Book*. These show capital and revenue items indiscriminately, including under expenditure all the costs of new canals and under revenue money borrowed as well as tolls. Such confusion reached a peak when proprietors were, on one occasion, paid £5 interest and asked for a £5 call,

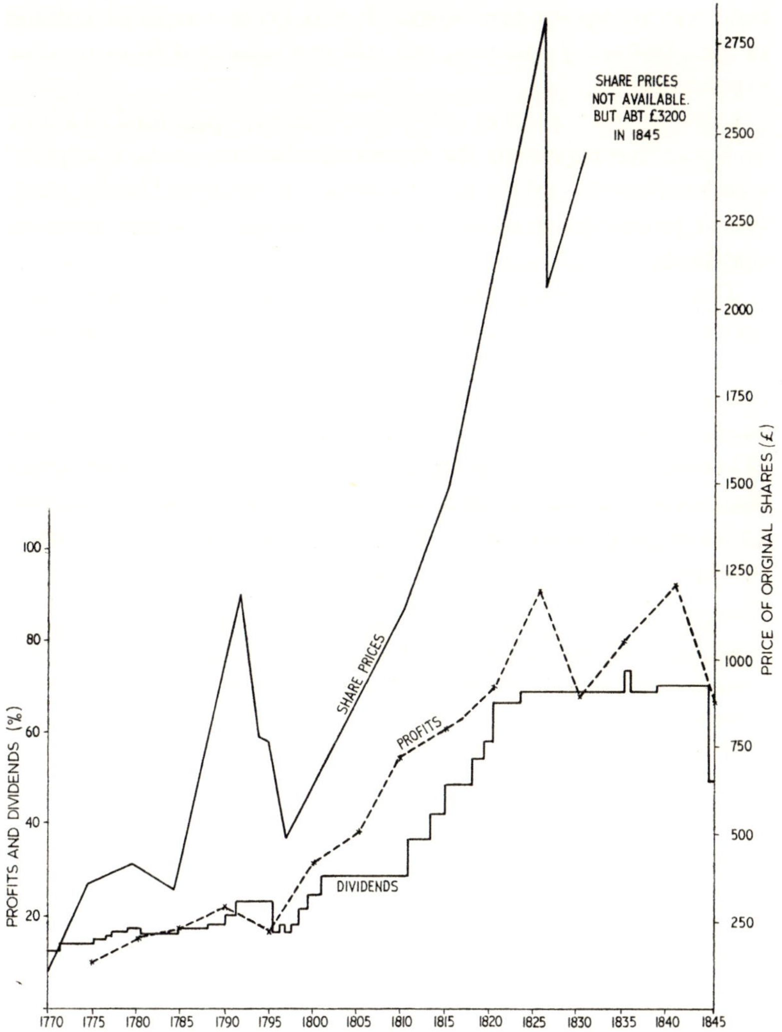

FIGURE 7. Diagram of profits, dividends and share prices, 1770–1845

the one to be offset against the other. The problem was not unknown to the committee, for the sub-committee of 1813 pointed out that dividends had not increased in proportion to tonnage because debt had been repaid and new works constructed 'which is so far a conversion of profits on tonnage into the Capital', but no suggestion was made of altering accounting methods.

However, the information given in these books is sufficiently sub-divided for us to rearrange it in modern form. This has been done for the *Abstracts* in Table II, which shows the profits at five-year intervals, and for the *Receipts and Expenditure* in Table III, which shows the total position for the three major divisions of our period. What is immediately visible is the high rates of profits to receipts, usually over one-half and sometimes approaching two-thirds, and the great excess of profits over dividends, accounted for by the fact that the two major periods of extension and rebuilding, 1785–1805 and 1825–35, were paid for entirely from profits, either directly or by borrowing money later repaid, and not by issuing more shares. It is also clear that there is little direct relationship between profits and dividends, the former fluctuating far more widely than the latter, to such an extent that the dividend in 1795, for example, could be met only by a substantial draft on reserves. One wonders, given the original arrangement of the accounts and the large cash balance in that year, whether the committee—or the treasurer—in fact realised that this was what they were doing.

Before 1800 profits exceeded dividends by £120,000, an average of 7 per cent of capital pa over the period in which dividends were being earned; between 1801 and 1825 the excess was £540,000 (nearly 30 per cent) and between 1826 and 1840 £130,000 (over 22 per cent). Once again behaving like a modern corporation, the company was determined to finance as much as possible of its expansion internally in order to maintain control and dividends.

How much it was prepared to risk in order to do this will be understood when it is realised that, apart from the loan from the Exchequer Loan Commissioners at the end of the twenties, which was for a fixed term, all loans were unfunded—ie they could be demanded back at short notice, usually three months. Moreover, by the end of the twenties the legal borrowing powers of the company had been exceeded, though an attempt at the General

Assembly of 1831 to prevent further borrowing was defeated. Nevertheless James Smallwood refused election to the committee in 1843 because the debt was not 'legalised'.

In January 1832 Freeth suggested what was to be the ultimate solution, to abolish the debt by 'making each Share responsible for a proportional part of the same'. This plan was adopted as the basis for a Parliamentary Bill at a General Assembly in September 1833 but there were not enough voting shares represented (after deducting the solicitor's proxies!) for the decision to be valid and the decision was not finally made until two years later. A Special Assembly in December 1835 subdivided the shares into 8,000 parts and allocated the whole debt (by then £568,000) in equal parts to each share at £71 per share. Those who did not pay this sum (and they appeared eventually to total about one-half the shares) would have interest deducted from their dividend. This interest has been deducted from the dividend whenever reference is made to the size of the latter in this book.

The major source of revenue was tonnage. This was fixed at 1½d per ton/mile by the first Act, and the company refused to reduce it, even suggesting that this was a minimum as well as a maximum. A request in 1797 to reduce the rate to ½d for certain inferior coals at Deepfield met the response that 'the Committee conceive themselves not authorised to make any partiality in the Rates on the Canal', though, in the hard times of the French Wars, they allowed wheat and flour to be navigated free from 8 November 1800 to 1 January 1801.

Letters requesting a reduction of tonnage were, in fact, a regular part of the business of committee meetings, especially at times of bad trade or increased competition. Except in the later years when action was sometimes taken because of railway competition, the committee pursued a consistent policy of refusal, whether to a suggestion from the Grand Junction and other canals suggesting reductions on heavy articles to attract traffic from the sea route via Gainsborough, to one from the Worcester & Birmingham suggesting reduced duties on clay to attract Potteries traffic from the Mersey or to requests from hard-pressed coalowners faced

Table II

A. *Half-yearly Trading and Profit and Loss*

Year (March)	1777	1780	1785	1790	1795	1800
Income						
Tonnage						
Rents						
Other						
Total Income	6,266	8,713	9,028	12,478	13,504	19,067
Expenditure						
Expenses	1,823	2,031	2,921	2,786	4,101	4,539
Interest	—	—	—	1,847	2,948	3,168
Net Profit c/d	4,443	5,882	6,107	7,845	6,455	11,360
Total Expenditure	6,266	8,713	9,028	12,478	13,504	19,067

B. *Half-yearly Appropriation and New Capital*

Year (March)	1777	1780	1785	1790	1795	1800
Net Profit b/d	4,443	5,882	6,107	7,845	6,455	11,360
Borrowing	—	—	5,500	14,100	2,310	—
Land Sold	—	—	—	—	—	—
From Reserves	211	—	970	—	5,669	—
Total Available	4,654	5,882	12,577	21,945	14,434	11,360
Dividends	3,426	4,428	4,200	6,300	9,450	6,300
Property Tax	—	—	—	—	—	—
Loans Repaid	1,030	—	4,000	—	—	—
Sinking Fund	—	—	—	—	—	—
Improvement Fund	—	—	—	—	—	—
Capital Improvements	198	528	4,377	14,595	4,984	1,747
To Reserves	—	926	—	1,050	—	3,313
Total Disbursed	4,654	5,882	12,577	21,945	14,434	11,360

Account of the BCN for selected years

1805	1810	1815	1820	1825	1830	(9 mths) 1835	1840	1845
23,023	32,601	37,887	43,194	46,582	49,036	77,320	61,008	61,820
183	197	286	410	301	211	—	—	713
84	84	120	147	400	—	—	203	—
23,290	33,382	38,293	43,751	47,283	49,247	77,320	61,271	62,533
6,704	10,956	14,523	17,739	14,147	14,001	19,891	17,478	19,907
2,510	1,749	907	—	—	11,764	27,902	10,437	18,196
14,076	20,577	22,873	26,012	33,136	23,482	29,527	33,356	24,430
23,290	33,382	38,293	43,751	47,283	49,247	77,320	61,271	62,533

Account of the BCN for selected years

1805	1810	1815	1820	1825	1830	(9 mths) 1835	1840	1845
14,076	20,577	22,873	26,012	33,136	23,482	29,527	33,356	24,430
—	—	—	—	—	—	21,277	34,600	8,046
—	—	—	900	—	1,104	5,546	—	—
—	—	—	7,590	24,195	39,762	—	—	27,839
14,076	20,577	22,873	34,502	57,331	64,348	56,350	67,956	60,215
10,500	1,050	15,000	21,000	25,000	25,000	25,000	33,130	28,472
—	—	2,744	—	—	—	—	—	—
—	—	—	—	—	4,850	—	—	—
1,200	1,600	—	—	—	—	—	—	—
—	—	2,000	10,015	10,000	5,178	—	—	—
2,052	3,441	2,831	3,497	22,331	29,320	26,824	27,843	31,743
324	5,036	298	—	—	—	4,526	6,983	—
14,076	20,577	22,873	34,502	57,331	64,348	56,350	67,956	60,215

I

TABLE III

Total profits and appropriations for the BCN 1767–1840
A. *Trading and Profit and Loss*

Period	1767–1800	1801–25	1826–40
Income	680,595	1,759,416	1,871,983
Expenditure:			
Salaries	43,112	89,851	110,745
Rent	}34,383	46,305	30,015
Taxes		108,820	68,361
Engines/Water	17,315	86,616	79,274
Repairs	57,968	213,109	110,666
Stationery & Incidents	5,706	18,005	17,413
Breaking Ice	3,081	5,149	2,925
Sundries	25,626	16,851	111,781
	187,191	584,706	531,180
Interest	70,699	67,365	385,237
Net profit c/d	422,705	1,107,345	955,566
Total	680,595	1,759,416	1,871,983

B. *Appropriation*

Period	1767–1800		1801–25		1826–40	
Net Profit b/d		422,705 (20%)		1,107,345 (63%)		955,566 (90%)
Dividends	303,165 (14%)		767,125 (43%)		734,053 (70%)	
Loans repaid	33,000		120,210		33,677	
Bilston Canal subscribers	2,941		7,018		—	
Surplus Fund			30,593		74,615	
New Works	83,599		182,399		113,321	
Total		422,705		1,107,345		955,566

C. Capital

Period	1767–1800		1801–25		1826–40	
Calls	70,025		—		—	
Loans	153,200		1,058		876,280	
From Revenue	83,599		182,399		113,321	
Total		306,824		183,457		989,601
Improvements:						
Land	22,741		26,092		11,738	
Parl. Expenses	19,199		18,335		13,025	
Works	252,634		97,922		883,968	
Total		294,574		142,349		908,731
Retained		12,250		41,108		80,780
Total		306,824		183,457		989,601

with competition from Forest of Dean coals in Oxford or ironmasters unable to compete with South Wales iron in London. When William Barker of Golden Hill Furnace, Newcastle (Staffs), requested a reduction of tonnage to enable him to bring ironstone thence to Birmingham, the committee resolved 'that the Interests both of the Comp^y & Mine Owners would be promoted by the export rather than the import of Iron Ore'.[13] Even when one Adams asked for a reduction 'to encourage the establishment of Stage Boats between Walsall and Wolverhampton to prevent such goods being taken to such Warehouse'[14] as was being erected at Bloxwich on the Wyrley Canal to collect goods by road and by-pass the BCN, he was refused. However, on rare occasions a reduction in tolls might benefit the company and was made, as when rates were reduced on coal going to the Coventry Canal. Faced by complaints by the Warwick & Birmingham Canal the committee said that their aim was 'to provide employment for numerous working colliers, Iron Makers and Labourers who deluged & have overburthened the Parishes (to the expence of which this Company are large contributors)'.[15]

The one concession that was eventually offered was annual

licensing, first suggested by the ironmaster J. T. Fereday in 1817 and incorporated in an Act the next year. However, this then opened the door for hard bargaining. Fereday had originally offered £1,000pa, but then demanded reduced rates and the final settlement was for £400pa. It was such bargaining problems that led the committee to severely restrict compounding only a few years later.

This was only one aspect of the problem of collecting tolls, which involved in particular the questions of credit and measurement. Early on the BCN decided upon a 'no credit' policy; in this they were followed by the other canals in the area, the Dudley Canal still refusing credit to 'Casual Boats' at the end of the century, though giving six months credit for all coals declared to be for stocking for winter use. By 1794, however, the BCN had agreed to allow credit from time to time to named traders, usually from week to week, but for three months for 'some of the principal and most responsible Traders . . . but the Co. having lately sustained some losses by this indulgence has induced them to come to the resolution of opening no new Accts without undeniable security for punctual payments'. By 1797 they were accepting 'Drafts on London quarterly instead of ready Money at the Toll Bars'.[16] Even before this, however, it appears that the company's servants had given credit on their own account, and, like the company later, had found difficulty in enforcing payment. In 1816, for example, the company bought ten iron boats from the Bradley iron works and then told them they had an account to settle which it would offset against the price!

Another problem was that of determining the amount due. At one stage the BCN were ready to give up and charge £1.75 per trip, irrespective of load, but this was almost immediately rescinded. Boats were gauged and painted in white capitals, but deception was still possible; coals, for example could be hidden under manure, which travelled free, boats were falsely gauged and had to be weighed and bills of lading were falsified. If all else failed, attempts were made to suborn the company's servants. On one occasion in 1772 a toll-clerk was asked to charge for half-a-ton less in each boat and as late as 1795 evidence was given that it was usual for boats which failed to find a cargo to avoid paying the minimum toll (which was for 20 tons) by giving 2s to the lockkeeper, while overweight boats might be passed when the lockkeeper 'has been purposely taken to and detained at a Public House'.

By 1842 the amount due on credit where the boats did not pass a toll office was being ascertained by inspection of the firm's books by 'three persons who are stationed along the line of the Canal and whose duty it is to watch and ascertain this traffic':

> All other Boats are gauged and the Amount of Tonnage is marked upon a [numbered] Ticket delivered up by the first Collector at whose station each boat arrives which ticket is exhibited and marked at every subsequent station ... & is delivered up at the last station ... All these tickets are monthly transmitted to the Office[17]

where the amount of tonnage due was calculated if credit was being allowed, it being collected at the last station in all other cases. All tickets were filed after checking and the sums taken by the collectors were collected at least three times each week and paid into the bank.

However, even when received safely, the tolls were subject to deduction. For decades the canal companies, not only in this area, fought a running battle with the local parish authorities to preserve their tolls from rating. At first the overseers of the poor demanded rates for land only, and it was a question only of the correct assessment, which was open to bargaining. In 1790, for example, the Birmingham overseers asked £30 for a 6d levy, were offered £24 and settled for £25. In 1792, however, they assessed the pumping engine at Broadwaters, an assessment they were able to maintain by reference to practice with mines engines.

Worse was to come. In 1793 Sedgeley overseers assessed the company on its profits. The committee were 'of opinion that the said Assessment is illegal & unprecedented & that no rate be therefore paid',[18] but a year later Harborne followed suit and the committee wrote to the Oxford and Coventry Canals to compare notes. The matter died down for a year or two but, following a repetition by Harborne in 1798, it was decided to take the matter to court, Quarter Sessions awarding in favour of the parish's lowest demand. Part of the matter at issue was the rating of 'dead' property such as bridges which 'were erected for public convenience & are rather nuisances than otherwise to the Navigation . . . no profit arises from the Locks'.[19] A circular was sent to other canals and meetings were held to discuss the promotion of a Bill in Parliament, but nothing was done at the time.

On 30 November 1804, however, the company received a demand for £40 10s (£40.50) from Wolverhampton overseers in place of the normal £6 18s 2½d (£6.91), together with a similar one from Bushbury. It was decided not to pay, but to reconvene a meeting of interested companies to discuss Parliamentary action. In the event Bushbury were paid, in return for a receipt stating that the money was a contribution to help the poor and not a payment of rates. The committee also decided to investigate the rates paid by '20 or 30 . . . of the most opulent & principal Traders in Wolverhampton . . . and the Turnpike Gates in that Township'.

In their letter to other canals the committee insisted 'that the Tolls are not Rents but profits in Trade', a dictum that the modern economist would find it hard to justify, and argued that

> From the utility of Canals they ought to be exempt from taxation as they tend to the emolument of the Parishes through which they run—increasing the value of the Lands, lowering the price of Fuel & other necessaries & furnishing many of the Poor with Employment[20]

Birmingham soon decided to levy rates on the same basis and the company elected delegates to a meeting in London to consider the matter. The Birmingham claim went to Warwick Quarter Sessions, the parish sub-poenaing so many of the company's agents on the line of the canal that, 'to prevent the waste of Water & other damages which might happen in their absence', the works had to be put under repair (ie closed). The result was a compromise; instead of the £250 demanded the company paid £100, but this was fixed for ever.

The Trent & Mersey Canal reported that they had counsel's opinion of the impossibility of a general derating Bill, but they thought it possible that one could be drawn up for a group of neighbouring canals. They were going ahead on these lines, including the Staffs & Worcs Canal and the BCN. In the end, however, following advice, they decided to go ahead alone. Meanwhile assessments continued to come in, that from West Bromwich being particularly troublesome; in spite of counsel's opinion it was decided not to pay. The company was called before a magistrate, lost its case and a warrant of distress was issued; timber belonging to the company was seized and they decided to pay up, seek a compromise and appeal. Meanwhile the West Bromwich parish officers employed a man to pay 3d to the steerers of all boats passing Rider's Green locks in return for a disclosure of their bills of lading and the Consistory Court of Lichfield excommunicated the company for non-payment of church rates!

So the war continued, with successes in some battles, losses in others, and constant bargaining and appeals to Quarter Sessions. In 1818, however, 'in consequence of two recent decisions in the Court of Kings Bench & two still more recent decisions in the Court of Quarter Sessions at Stafford'[21] it was decided not to pay any future poor rates levied on tolls. Rate reductions followed all round—Tipton from £21 to £5, Bloxwich from £10 18s 8d (£10.93½) to £2 10s (£2.50), but other parishes went to court. In the end Warwick Sessions decided that tolls should be rated *pro rata* to the length of canal in the parish, locks as land and bridges not at all. Costs were £1,200. For all practical purposes the war was lost and the company concentrated on getting the best terms it could from all its opponents.

THE COAL TRADE

Tonnage was not always the only source of revenue, though it was by far the largest. Apart from a few rents, for the first decade and a half of its existence the BCN engaged itself in the coal trade.

As early as October 1769 it was resolved that 'till the last Friday in March next' they should buy coal and carry it to the wharves and to different parts of the town,

> and it is desir'd they will take care to make a Profit thereon over and above every contingent Expence, & £5 per Cent Interest on the money employ'd But that such profit do not exceed One farthing per Hundred on the Coal.[22]

It was decided to sell in small lots at the bulk rate to benefit the poor.

A sub-committee was set up to deal with the business, but it was decided to set up a separate fund, 'no part of the Company's Property [being] appropriated as Security to the Persons who advance the Money'. Provision was made for a fleet of fifty boats though this order was later suspended and, apparently, forgotten. Dr Ash felt that this venture into trade was necessary

> for ye advantage of the Public as the only means of keeping down the price of Coals; without which the private owners of Boats would never have sold Coals any cheaper than the Waggons had used to do than merely to gain the preference,

and so that 'every *apprehension* of Monopoly be totally removed',[23] As we have seen, not everyone agreed with this view; the decision to continue the trade in March 1770 was carried only by 278–132, but the General Assembly agreed 'to take a Mine not exceeding forty Acres . . . professedly with no view of working the said Mine, unless and untill a combination in the Coal masters . . . shall make it appear . . . necessary'.[24]

Coal was purchased at 4s 4d (21½p) per ton of 21cwt from Wednesbury and at 3s 4d (16½p) from Bilston, the coalowner asking for a loan of £300 to develop the latter. In general there seems to have been some trouble in obtaining sufficient coal, though it is not clear whether this was because of the price offered (which seemed to leave a large margin for profit when sold) or because the coalowners feared being squeezed out. Certainly one problem was that the coalowners seemed to have little capital for expansion. The necessity for loans has been mentioned, and the contract with one Bickley laid it down that he should have £50 per week regularly, with accounts balanced the first Monday in each month.

This latter contract was the cause of some trouble. Soon after it was made Bickley announced that he could send only three boat-loads per week and also refused to weigh by any machine other than his own. An attempt was made, without success, to find other sources of supply, and it was then found that he sold coal more cheaply to the company's competitors. As a result the company's boats were cut off and he was forced to reduce his price to 3s 2d (16p) per ton; not surprisingly it was found 'that there is a much greater quantity of Small & Sleck in each boat than there might be & the weight very deficient'.[25]

In general the price paid seems to have been under 3s 6d (17½p) per ton, sometimes with an extra payment for loading into the boats, though this obviously depended on quality. Gilbert Fownes, for example, was paid 3s 9¾d (19p) on a three-year contract, but he guaranteed that no coals would be of less than 21lb.*

At first the coal was sold at 8s 4d (41½p), soon reduced to 7s 6d (37½p) and then to 6s 8d (33½p), where it remained for some time, being reduced to 6s 4d (31½p) in the middle of 1774. As a result other carriers were forced to follow suit. The Birmingham Boat Company, for example, advertised

> in order to invalidate what has been maliciously propagated, namely that they (as some Individuals do) will take every Opportunity to advance the Price of Coal, think it indispensibly necessary to reiterate what they before promised, viz. That they (and they only) now do and are determined to continue selling at 4d per Hundred[26]

The committee used 'all Boats which [could] be spared from the Business of the Navigation' and hired more from outside. These boats were let out to contractors, who provided all necessary materials except towing poles and rudders and agreed to raise any

* I.e. no lump would weigh less than 21lb

sunken boats at their own expense, each man to be accountable for his own boat. The agreed price was 10d per mile. In addition four persons were contracted with to unload at 2d per ton. For a 25-ton boat, this is just under 7d per ton expenses, or a profit of about 2s 8d (13½p) per ton—over 1½d per hundredweight rather than a farthing!

The money involved in the trade was considerable, receipts averaging around £2,500 pa at the peak (1777–83) and totalling £20,165 over the whole period of the trade. (Unfortunately there are no separate Coal Trade Accounts surviving to allow us to estimate profits). However this suggests only 150 tons per week at the beginning of the period, so that the company remained a minority interest, though a substantial one.

There was some problem with dishonesty. The first weigh-machine attendant had to be dismissed because he took bribes, and his successor, who was paid 12s (60p) per week with 3s (15p) per week extra, 'provided he behaves himself to the satisfaction of the Committee', eventually went the same way because of deficiencies in his accounts. Coal purchasers were told not to pay more than 2d per ton to the men for drink and to report any who demanded more. Steerers were

> obliged to sign an Article that they [would] not unload any Coal out of the Boats in their passage from the pits, except when the Water [was] low, to get over a sill & then, as soon as they [were] over, that they [would] again reload them into the Boats,

with a penalty of £1 for disobedience. All boats had to be brought at least half a mile the Birmingham side of Oldbury before being moored, 'nor shall be suffer'd to lie all night within less than half a Mile of any Village', for fear of pilfering.[27]

As the company's trade reached its peak, opposition reappeared. It was reported that private boat-owners sent out their servants to hire carts on the way to the wharf to prevent the company getting its coal away and combinations were made between coalowners and private traders to prevent renewal of the company's coal contracts. Rumours were circulated as to the quality of the company's coals; 'A LOVER OF TRUTH' alleged that they had 'contracted for a large Quantity of Coals entirely the Refuse of other Coal Dealers, at a very considerable Abatement in Price, and which have lain in the Field twelve Months or upwards', and accused them of underselling others because their clerks' wages and boat overheads were not charged to the trade.[28]

Perhaps as a result of this opposition, the matter was reopened in the company and a decision taken (300–27) to continue the trade but (by 217–69) to discontinue the separate committee. The trade continued for another four years, notwithstanding renewed complaints by other coal dealers that the company had too many boats in competition. These were in fact, the peak years for receipts. In 1780, however, the committee recommended to the General Assembly that the trade be discontinued and the boats hired out, but the recommendation was referred back. In 1783, at the time of the Parliamentary manoeuvring about the Fazeley Canal, it was agreed with the Staffs & Worcs Canal, as the price of their neutrality, to discontinue the trade and it finally ceased on 1 July 1784. It was handed over to Mrs Hipkiss, the widow of the company's wharfinger, provided she paid interest on the debt to the company which she inherited from her husband.[29]

It had certainly served its purpose of expanding trade. By 1800 a local rhymster could report:

> They visited our WHARFS, and, wand'ring found
> Some thousand tons of COAL pil'd on the ground,
> And scores of boats, in length full sixty feet,
> With loads of mineral fuel, quite replete,
> Whilst carts, and country waggons, fill'd each space,
> And loaded teams stood rang'd around the place.[30]

and in 1824, 'A County Gentleman' reported that from just one direction, 'There pass on the canal about fifty boats a day from the direction of Birmingham and, of course, as many towards that place'[31]—or enough to keep the locks in use for nearly nine hours each day.

CHAPTER 7

Maintenance and Operation

MAINTENANCE

Such a trade required large quantities of water, and we have seen the efforts required to obtain it. Equal effort was required to retain it, especially since those who dwelt or worked near the canal saw it not only as a purveyor of transport but also as a source of water. Colliery owners, for example, sought assistance in fighting fires by flooding their pits, though such water was often returned by the pumping engines to the canal. Once the new Boulton & Watt engines came into use there were requests for canal water for condensing, which could require considerable quantities. The problems was to ensure that such condensing water was returned to the canal, since it involved the necessity of pumping it back rather than letting it flow away by gravity. Losses grew so severe that, on the motion of Samuel Tertius Galton, following a report by Watt, the General Assembly resolved that in all case where injection water did not run back into the canal by gravity,

> no Drain whatever shall be permitted [for injection water] except into a Water-tight shallow Pit or Cistern from whence it shall be raised by a Pump erected and maintained at the Expence of the Proprietors of the said Engine . . . which Pump shall return all such Water . . . into the Canal above high Water Level.[1]

There were, of course, always those who would take what they wanted without worrying about permission. In July 1820 one of the company's servants 'was violently assaulted whilst in the act of repairing a Course which conveys the Birm^m Coal Comp^ys Engine Water into the Canal . . . by Isaac Norton who has frequently diverted such water to supply his Father's whimsy with condensing water'.² John Haycock, a steerer, gave an account of another incident, in 1798:

> On Tuesday night last they were taking in Nails . . . at a Bridge near Mr Wilkinsons Works at Bradley called the Slitting Mill Bridge—at about Seven o'Clock [he] saw a tallish man come with a Shovel & begin digging in the Bank of the Canal on the Towing path side & opened a valve or Sough through which the Canal Water flowed very fast & continued running when they came away between Nine & ten o'Clock . . . when they arose the Morning their Boat was aground & lay on one side the Boats on Tuesday morning could not pass.³

This was merely a blatant incident in a continuing war against 'truncks'—channels by which water could be drawn off unknown to the company. They were particularly common in private basins, being used to draw the water off when the basin needed cleaning; one careless use of such a 'plug' to clean Aston's basin, which lowered the canal some inches, precipitated a minute banning all such devices. Nevertheless such contrivances were estimated to be causing the loss of 200 locksful weekly in 1797, and gave constant trouble to the company's officers. In one instance, however, blame lay elsewhere. In February 1821

> Thomas Norton observed two men at Work cutting the Embankment of the Canal at Ettingwall which is ten feet above the Ground level . . . upon examination it was found to have been opened three broad and two feet deep up to & partly into the Puddle & supposed to be by Colliers who refuse working at the late reduced wages with intent to deluge the Collieries & prevent others having employment.⁴

A main source of water to supply the canal was, as has been seen, the mines pumping engines. Later Acts gave the companies the right to all water pumped out by mines served by the canals—though that from mines bordering canals built under earlier Acts had still to be paid for, and in the later cases the additional cost had to be met of raising water to canal level. By 1813 there were forty engines raising water to the summit of the BCN, of which the company paid only for three, totalling £266. In total the engines raised 340 locksful per day. From 1825 there are annual lists of engines lifting water into the BCN, which show the number pumping to the summit to vary from twenty-two to forty, averaging over thirty (of which, eventually, six belonged to the company). They delivered 40–60,000 locksful each year, the major part of this being accounted for by the company's engines, the others never providing over 15,000 locksful, at a cost never more than £200. A similar number pumped to the Walsall level, where the company had no engines, providing 11–15,000 locksful at a similar cost.

The company's engines, of course, cost far more, and the cost increased. Between 1780 and 1804 the cost ranged from £162 to £2,097 yearly, with only four years exceeding £1,000; from 1803–14 the range was from £2,220 to £4,952 and by the 1820s it was running at over £5,000, a matter which caused considerable concern to the Accounts Committee. It remained at that level for the rest of our period.[5]

One engine that caused considerable trouble was that at Ashted. For one thing, the Ashted and Aston locks were so heavily used that any interruption of the engine's working could have serious results. On a day in late August 1814, for example, William Buxton, who was in charge of that engine, did not get to work until 8 am, with the result that the Hospital Pond ran dry. (This was not the only complaint about Buxton; in 1818 Murdock reported his engine as being badly kept and Buxton's 'conduct and expressions ... upon the occasion of Mr Murdocks observations' were such as to 'promise no expectation of improvement in his conduct'. He was sacked).[6]

On the other hand, however, if the engineman were zealous for the trade he could overpump from the lower pound. Gauges were fixed to prevent this in 1803, following complaints from the Warwick & Birmingham company; in 1811 it was found that a piece of timber had been 'nailed or otherwise fastened' on to the weir at the BCN side of the junction to divert the water over the Warwick company's weir. By 1819 matters had been made worse because the two enginemen concerned were not on good terms: 'Jukes [of the BCN] had allowed upon one occasion his tongue an unwarrantable license'. However it was alleged that the Warwick Canal wanted to take more than their share in order to avoid drawing upon their reservoir and were threatened that the BCN might 'take measures to separate the Waters which would injure the Warwick Canal'.[7] Three years later the Warwick Canal were alleging in their turn that boats were being grounded 'in consequence of the Water being drawn too low' as a result of 'the ardour of the Men who work the Engines'.[8] It was agreed that the engines should pump, not from the canal but from reservoirs replenished over weirs.

Water alone was not enough, however; depth had to be maintained by the prevention of silting, caused both by bank subsidence and by coals and other things going overboard and off the banks. The problem, until suitable dredgers had been invented (and then there was danger to the puddle) was that, to cleanse the bottom, the canal had to be closed, with consequent disruption. Throughout September 1796, for example, there was an angry exchange of letters between the Birmingham Canal and the Staffs & Worcs about the stoppage then in progress, the former arguing that, 'considering the season of the Year and the difficulty of procuring proper Hands in the Harvest, there has been as much dispatch given to the work as possible' and that the injury was not 'to be compared with the benefitts [to be] derived from it in future'.[9]

Because of the problems involved such work was often put off and resort had to expedients:

> Some Years ago the Weirs of the Canal were rais'd to the utmost height that the Works would admit and the depth of the Water thereby increas'd which gave a temporary relief to the Trade—But no method now remains but . . . the removing the filth and mud from the bottom.[10]

By the end of our period such stoppages were co-ordinated. Each year Pickfords would, for example, 'inform their friends and the public that the Annual Stoppage of Canals for repairs will commence on Monday 25th instans and continue one week'.[11]

One cause was that 'the Banks . . . are too upright . . . they form a harbour for vermin and are thereby & by the lashing of the water under min'd, and . . . thrown down into the water'.[12] Though several remedies were tried, none was successful until the Telford rebuilding when vertical banks were lined throughout with brick. Other causes, then as now, included 'the Rubbish thrown in by the Children' and 'Coping Stones . . . thrown off several of the Canal Bridges'.[13] In 1804 the canal was stopped three days by a boat sunk under a bridge by two boatmen 'striving wch should first pass the said Bridge'.[14] On one occasion, when Mr T. Eyre Lee observed Joshua Collins 'throwing bats & Rubbish out of a Boat . . . into the Canal' he was taken to the magistrate, fined 50p and dismissed from his employment, but many offenders were on a larger scale, as with 'vast quantities of Furnace Cinders . . . which . . . have been boated from the different works and clandestinely deposited' in the canal.[15]

As a result the canal was often in a 'very shallow & foul state'. At one time, 'Near Winson Green the Canal [was] so filled up and the Channel so narrow as to admit in some places of only one loaded boat passing at a time'.[16] In 1805 the company's engineer conferred with William Murdock 'in respect to the possibility & propriety of constructing a moveable Steam Engine to draw the Water out of the Canal for the purpose of effecting the repair of the Works . . . without loss of Water', and this resulted in a 'Machine for throwing Water over a Dam of pile planks in order that the repair of the Works may be effected in the Summer Season without loss of water'.[17] It cost £878. Later, Murdock gave it as his opinion that 'a Machine may be constructed to clear Mud & filth out of the Canal without drawing out the Water'.[18] He was given the go ahead and produced a model which was approved. As a result a full-scale 'mudding machine' in an iron

Page 149 Horses and locks: (*above*) horse-drawn tar-boat owned by Thomas Clayton of Oldbury entering top lock, Spon Lane, 1955; (*below*) day-boat with unorthodox hauling 'mast' approaching Perry Barr top lock on its way to Hamstead colliery, 1956

Page 150
(*left*) Lamp standard, Farmer's Bridge, probably erected around 1800, disused when traffic no longer necessitated night work;

(*right*) Riders Green locks. The square tower in the background is a wooden cooling tower

hull was produced and ready to work by the end of 1815, but it did not prevent closures.

A big problem for any canal in a mining area was, of course, subsidence. In January 1798, for example, the south end of Dudley tunnel was in danger of collapse as a result of coal working by Messrs Hawkes and Badley; in the same year Hood reported 'that amongst the Colliery's the Banks and the Towing paths of the Canal continue to sink & require considerable quantities of Earth to keep them up' and a few years later that 'a Bridge over the Canal near Wednesbury new Colliery is sunk so low that the Boat Horses cannot pass under it'.[19]

In 1802, the committee 'considering the Canal and Works in danger of material injury from the imprudence of the Miners in taking the Coals from under',[20] decided to take counsel's opinion as to who was liable for repairs arising from subsidence. His report being favourable proceedings were commenced against several mineowners, but this did not end the problem. Only a few years later one of the Toll End locks had sunk a foot and the mineowners responsible stated calmly 'that such Lock would sink four or five feet below its original level but by cautiously working the Mine they had no doubt of its being kept upright'![21] Others gave notice that they were about to open a pair of old pits so near one of the Tipton Green locks that there would be 'no road for the Boat Horses & they conceive that the Towing Path must be made on the other side of the Canal'.[22]

When the mineowners were forced to do repairs they often did them badly:

> The Summit from Tipton Green to Monmoor Green instead of being upon a level with the adjoining Land as formerly is become an unbroken Chain of Embankments ... in many instances where the Canal Banks have been raised & repaired by the Mine Owners & improper Materials used ... there are considerable leakages & want of Strength in the Embankments.[23]

The trouble was that the law was slow and profits both certain and considerable, so working under the canal continued, though

K

usually some compensation was gained, if only by threatening to close the relevant colliery branch.

This was not all there was to maintenance. A constant check had to be kept on the state of the canal, from lock gates—in 1822 the top gate of the third Aston lock was 'expected to break down every Day'—to serious mishaps or even disasters. 1798-9 seems to have been a year of heavy rains, and they took their toll. On 15 February 1799 the bank of the canal gave way near Ladywood

> When a number of empty boats were carried into the valley. It fortunately happened that the breach was made by the water in the bank on the upper side, and that the falling earth completely stopped the culvert, and dammed up the water in the valley, or great damage must have been done to the lower part of the town.[24]

In May the embankment of the Warwick & Birmingham Canal at Bordesley gave way, flooding the meadows below and putting some houses 4ft under water. At the 'ice flood in 1795' the reservoir of Robert Peel's cotton mill at Drayton burst 'and poured down the ice on the arches of the aqueduct ... It cut the faces of the wing walls more than a brick deep, and tore the arch as far as the water could force the ice into it'. The aqueduct was repaired 'in haste ... of Old Canal Boats'[25] and not rebuilt in brick until 1825.

To deal with such matters required organisation. In 1801 houses were erected at strategic points for the accommodation of labourers who had to be ready to turn out at all hours in time of flood, but from the early years attempts had been made to let the regular maintenance out to contract. Advertisements appeared in May 1774 for 'a person to undertake the Repair of the Towing Paths and Fences, at a certain Rate per Mile',[26] the final agreement, with Jno Partridge, being for £2 10s (£2.50) per mile. This did not, however, last long, and two years later the company took over its own maintenance, employing its erstwhile contractor at 2s (10p) per day. Some years later, a sub-committee appointed to review employment policy reported in favour of the contract

MAINTENANCE AND OPERATION 153

system. Advertisements were inserted for tenders for annual contracts to repair all works except those of stone, brick, timber and iron, which were maintained by the company's own staff—mainly the lock-keepers. There were six contracts. They are shown below with the tenders, those accepted being marked by an asterisk.

1. Autherley to Gospel Oak £136. £90.*
2. Gospel Oak to Spon Lane, including the Ocker Hill Branch and Titford Reservoir £130. £134 10s.*
3. Spon Lane to end of both upper branches at Birmingham, including Smethwick and Birmingham Heath reservoirs. £134. £132 8s. £123.*
4. Farmer's Bridge to Minworth with the Digbeth Branch. £207. £131 (none accepted?).
5. Minworth to Fazeley (no offer).
6. Fazeley to Whittington Brook. £82 10s.*

As far as can be seen this system endured virtually unchanged, with additions and modifications as new lengths were built, until 1831, when the contracts were allowed to lapse, more men employed for maintenance and the canal divided into three 'regions'. The cost of maintenance of course rose. By 1810 Aston to Marston Field cost £285 and Marston Field to Whittington Brook £283, the contractors having the lock-houses and looking after the locks. By this time one year's payment was required as security. Nevertheless, there were problems; in 1814 William Piddock, the walking surveyor, complained he had suffered 'gross insult and abuse' from the men employed by the contractor Samuel Hodgkinson on the Ocker Hill embankment. Hodgkinson was told this would be his last contract. By 1821 the total cost of the contracts was £1,365.50, falling to £1,243 the next year—though the total repairs bill was £13,898 in 1820 and £14,518 in 1821. As a result of the activities of the Accounts Committee this had fallen to £5,327 for the half-year ending July 1824 and averaged around £7,500 yearly at the end of our period, when the contracts had ended and Telford's reconstruction had presumably made maintenance easier.

OPERATION

Some of the boats which navigated the canal were provided by the company, most by private traders. The earliest were 'day boats' of a type used on the canal as long as commercial carrying lasted. They were 'long and carr[ied] from 25 to 30 tons, . . . drawn by a single horse . . . at the rate of about two miles an hour'.[27] As through traffic grew long-distance boats appeared from other canals, often owned by the big carriers such as Hugh Henshall whose advertisements were soon to be found in the Birmingham papers. Until the end of the period the crew was usually a man and a boy and families did not, apparently, live on the boats.

Standardisation came early, encouraged, indeed enforced, by the company's regulations, often designed to save water by ensuring the maximum load through the locks. As a result, so Hutton reported, 'the boats are nearly alike, constructed to fit the locks'. He continued:

> each [is] drawn by something like the skeleton of a horse, covered with skin; whether he subsists on the scent of the waters, is a doubt; but whether his life is a scene of affliction is not; for the unfeeling driver has no employment but to whip him from one end of the canal to the other.[28]

The canal was the scene of some of the earliest experiments with iron boats. John Wilkinson's first iron boat came up the canal soon after launching

> loaded with 22 tons 15 hundredweight of its own metal . . . the thickness of the plates with which it is made is about 3-16ths, and it is put together with rivets, like coppers, or fire engine boilers: but the stern-posts are wood, and the gun whale is lined with, and the beams made of, elm planks.[29]

She weighed 8 tons, drew 8 or 9in when light and carried 32 tons. By the end of the century Wilkinson was using such boats in ordinary trade.

MAINTENANCE AND OPERATION 155

A request in 1816 from Joshua Horton for permission 'to work a Steam passage boat between Wolverhampton and Birmingham' was however, refused, the committee feeling 'that great inconvenience to the Trade & damage to the Works may arise therefrom'.[30]

Boats, of course, needed wharves and other facilities, and the struggle over the wharves at the terminal has already been described. The company provided warehouses at its wharves, 'Coak' sheds, with slate roofs (the slate itself brought by canal), and even an eight-day clock, besides accommodation for their employees. As trade grew the wharf at Brickkiln Piece was enlarged to a 'bason', and that at Wolverhampton was made wide enough for four boats to unload and three to lie abreast.

In addition, wharves were opened by other persons; in 1774 Roger Eyhyn opened a wharf at Wolverhampton 'on the Turnpike Road leading to Willenhall' and Badger's wharf, 'with a large and commodious Warehouse thereon' was opened 'within a hundred Yards of the Birmingham Navigation-Office at the bottom of Rottens Row in Wolverhampton' at which Henshall's called, 'the first of any wharf upon the Birmingham Canal'.[31] From 14 May 1774 Henshall sent a regular boat every Saturday at 6 am from Birmingham, arriving at Manchester and Liverpool the following Saturday, for £2 12s 6d (£2.62½) per ton—a price reduced to £1 10s (£1.50) by 1777 when the Trent & Mersey Canal was opened along its full length.

Not only were Birmingham's products taken out; new products were brought in, including 'Any quantity of good "BURTON ALE" "WHITBREADS' long-famed LONDON PORTER", and fine SLATES . . from Westmoreland and Wales'.[32] The list could be continued indefinitely.

By the end of the century traders were asking for better facilities. In 1797 Thomas Sherratt, having gained permission for his proposed fly-boats to pass at night, tried to get extended lock opening times for ordinary boats. After some refusals it was agreed to open them fourteen hours each day, 'when there is sufficient light either Morning or Evening for Boats to pass without damage to the Works'.[33] He was also allowed to pass locks on nine consecutive Sundays to carry urgent merchandise to London. Such problems became more urgent as fly-boat traffic increased, and by 1810 permission was being granted to their operators to pass boats 'at all times'. By 1819 this was regular practice, it being necessary specially to inform carriers in time of drought 'that Night Boats & Sunday Boats could not be indulged with passage until a supply of Water could be obtained'.[34]

On one occasion in 1804 special facilities were offered Matthew Boulton to carry between £200,000 and £300,000 of silver dollars he had minted for Ireland, in two boats with twelve soldiers and two Bow Street Runners. The way was cleared by day and night:

> To prevent the Crowd of Boats which are frequently lying at Farmers Bridge the Locks at Smethwick were not opened on Thursday morning ... until Nine O'Clock—the boats which had arrived at Farmers Bridge the preceding night were all passed at ten O'Clock when the Boats laden with Dollars arrived there—... they cleared the Aston locks by four—were at Preston Brook ... at four in the evening of Saturday And at Liverpool at two o'Clock the morning following.[35]

Farmer's Bridge locks were a particular bottleneck, with frequent complaints of delay. In 1801 they were opened from 9 to 10 am on Sundays during the short days to clear traffic and the next year a 'small Office' was built at the top (it is still there) for a man 'constantly to attend to pass [boats] in their proper turns and thereby prevent the obstructions and delays'.[36] In 1803 'Six Active Men' were employed 'to expedite the passage of Boats', but even they were not enough, and consideration had to be given to night work. Lamps were ordered for the stretch between Farmer's Bridge and Snow Hill in 1802 but two years later it was still necessary to order 'that Iron Hand Rails be fix'd on the upper Gates of the Locks [at] Farmers Bridge ... to enable the Steerers to pass their Boats in the Night without Lamps'[37] and the matter of lamps came up again in 1807. By 1815 the question of gas lighting was being considered and three years later an estimate was received of £594 for 25 lamps an annual charge of £95.50. Next year an estimate of £495 was received for a gasometer, 'and considering that inconvenience may arise from a Gasometer placed in the Cos Timber Yard', the Gas Company was asked to supply lights. This they did for £5.25 per lamp pa for 21 lamps for 14 years. The original lights were 'common Round Lamps' which did not give sufficient light and were replaced by square ones.

Similar problems arose at Fazeley, where boats were stopped during the hours of service on Sunday which was 'the cause of much confusion & tumult—sometimes 20 to 30 being collected together all striving to be first the fly's with 2 Horses each! It was agreed in 1821 that this hindrance should be removed, and the next year to allow night passage—'well worth the additional expence of Water & Lockkeepers to induce the Fly Trade'.[38] However, at the same time it was decided not to open Wolverhampton locks at night at the request of Crowley & Co., 'it appearing . . . that the Trade of the District does not require or other Carriers call for such extra exertion & indulgence which would give such Boats an undue preference and create dissatisfaction'.[39]

All canal companies tried to control and speed the trade by various regulations. The Wyrley & Essington Canal, for example, adopted an exhaustive list of twenty-two by-laws in 1795. Of these three were concerned with the important matter of water supply. Number thirteen, for instance, which carried a penalty of 40s to £5, ordered that

> every Boatman . . . shall before he opens the Gates of any Lock examine the paddles and Valves and see that the Water in and below the Lock is of the same Level . . . nor shall at any time when the Boat is in a Lock and the Water sunk level with the Lower Canal open the upper valve to force the Boat out of the Lock nor shall he suffer his boat to go out of the lock till he has let down the Lower Valves and when out shut close the lower Gates.[40]

In general, the regulations for avoiding obstructions and disputes, of which there were thirteen, carried lesser penalties, varying from 25p to £2. Boats had to travel at not less than 2mph nor more than 8mph without attempting to overtake, each being drawn by one horse only which was to be fastened, when the boat was moored, by a halter not more than 2yd long, and not to eat the hedges. It was a felony to damage the banks and no one was to rake for coals, for fear of damaging the puddle, 'excepting the owners of Coals navigated on the Canal'. It would appear that boats did not have bow fenders, because the boatman was ordered to guide his boat 'as gently as possible into the Lock and also at such times be prepared with a Lever or piece of Wood which he shall put between the Locks and the fore end of the Boat to prevent the Boat striking against the Lock'.[41] It was a serious crime, punishable with a fine of up to £5, to float timber on the canal or tip ballast into it.

These regulations were typical, being based on the experience to date of other canals in the area. The Dudley Canal had, in addition, regulations of some complexity for working through tunnels, which at one time for some reason permitted entry into the east end of Lapal tunnel between 12 noon and 4 pm or 12 midnight and 4 am but into the west end only between 8 and 8.30 am or 6 and 6.30 pm.

The Birmingham Canal had adopted various by-laws, basically of a similar nature, but found them difficult to enforce. As early as May 1770 'Mr Meredith reported to the Cttee that he had apply'd to several of the Owners of the private Boats respecting Offences agst the Bye Laws of the Comp. from some of whom he received Contemptious answers'[42] and it was found that the cost of obtaining convictions was often greater than the penalty. It was therefore suggested that all penalties be £5, with power of mitigation, and be imposed on owners, since servants were not usually householders and were thus 'screened' from a Warrant of Distress. It was, in fact, found better to incorporate regulations in subsequent Acts of Parliament:

> We have derived very little if any advantage from the bye-laws—there has always been a Backwardness in the Magistrates to act upon them—in 1784 Parliamentary Powers were obtained which we

have found much more Effective than all Bye Laws & which the Magistrates have upon all occasions enforced.[43]

Nevertheless the company did make regulations for the good government of the canal, by minute rather than bye-law, such as that boats must not be permitted to enter a lock 'without an able Horse and able and experienced Hands to navigate the same' and the constantly reiterated orders against 'the indecent Practice of Bathing' especially in view of the fact that the towing-path had 'become a Public Walk'.[44]

One ever-present problem was that of violent disorder, as when three of Pickford's boatmen 'threw nearly one half of the Coping . . . Stones off one side of a Public Road Bridge . . . into the Canal . . . to retard some Boat or Boats they expected to meet or follow them & as a cover for some neglect or wilfull delay'. One steerer,

> by violently forcing His Boat against the Stone Work of a Swivel Bridge . . . forced four large Stones & Brick Work with the Timber & Land ties out of their places & has rendered the Bridge impassable & in order to force his way thro' a lock after the Hours of Navigation He endeavour'd to break open the padlock which he could not easily effect but in order to fill the lock . . . chip'd the edges of the Square Quoin of the Lock in order that the Water might pass thro' the apperture & by that & forcing the Gate with an Iron Craw He fill'd the Lock & pass'd thro' it.[45]

If disorder was common, pilfering was endemic. A £21 reward for the conviction of the person stealing 30cwt of lead off the buildings on the wharf only drew attention to one of the more flagrant cases; in 1820 the gas-lamp pipes were stolen and losses of coal from boats were perpetual. On one occasion the carpenter was found to have 'devoted much of his time & the Company's Timber to his own purposes' and on another 'a Tonnage Ticket . . . was laid before the Committee & the field Ticket from which the same was made by which it appears that the Tonnage Ticket hath been altered from 20 tons 10 Ct to 22.10 with intent to defraud' the purchaser of the coals. The company appointed watchmen and supported various societies for the suppression of theft and the prosecution of felons, but the problem was unending. On 21 December 1789 Bull, the company's engineer, who lived in the Smethwick lock-house,

> was awoke by a violent wrenching of the house doors, and a battery of the walls; he immediately arose ... and opened a window ... when a large brick was thrown at him, and soon followed by thirteen other pieces of brick and stone.

He retired and the men broke in and ransacked the lower rooms, then, forcing open the bedroom door,

> three men having handkerchiefs across their faces approached him, with pistols and iron-bars in their hands ... They compelled Mr and Mrs Bull to stand with their faces to the wall while they broke open a bureau, and stripped the room of everything they could carry away, the bed-clothes, &c. not excepted.[47]

Fifty guineas reward was offered and three men were arrested, sentenced to death and hanged.

THE LABOUR FORCE

Like all canals, the Birmingham Canal had a high capital/labour ratio. By the end of our period capital per man employed was in the region of £30,000 and profits per man were around £300, figures which would be the envy of many big firms today, in spite of the decline in the value of money during the last century. The ratio of capital costs, at current interest rates, to current expenses, ranged from one to two at the beginning of the Canal's existence to three to one in 1846. Income was, however, much more akin to that received by a landowner renting out his property than to the profits of a modern firm and the labour force was mainly occupied in maintaining and extending the network and on supervising the collection of revenue.

In the central office there was a clerk, or chief officer, with three or four assistants. There were wharfingers at the company's wharves at Birmingham, Wolverhampton and Fazeley, each with up to four clerk/assistants, nightwatchmen and, perhaps, some

MAINTENANCE AND OPERATION 161

loaders. There were also an increasing number of lock-keepers, with supervisors at the three stop-locks. For maintenance there was the superintendent and the engineer, with at various times some 'walking surveyors'. Apart from contractors for the various districts, this was the total work force, except when new works were being constructed. During our period those directly employed probably never exceeded sixty in normal times. These it is now proposed to pass in review.

The chief executive at the Navigation Office was the clerk—at first the solicitor, Meredith, who was not a good choice, since he was virtually part-time and confusion arose as to the fees he could charge. He was replaced by John Houghton in 1787, at a salary of £200pa, raised to £300 with £100 annual gratuity in 1803. In 1817 he was given a share in the company. Houghton remained clerk until his death in 1825 when he was succeeded by John Freeth, who had been his deputy for many years and who retained the post until 1844.

The clerk was assisted by a small clerical force, who were expected to work from 8 am to 7 pm with an hour for lunch, reduced in 1811 to 9 am–7 pm with one and a half hours lunch and in 1842 to 9.30 am to 4 pm. There was a principal accountant, appointed at £150pa, later assisted by a 'first Bookkeeping Clerk' at £84 and a second at £63. The first to hold this latter post was John Houghton. Freeth was added to the establishment as a clerk in 1791 and there was little change thereafter until the increased traffic after 1830 made increased staff essential. Two other clerks were appointed in 1826 and Freeth's salary was raised to £500 in 1835. In 1839 his assistant was given £300pa; at this date there were also a 'Collector and Paymaster of Workmen' and a cashier, both of whom received £250 (and had to give sureties for £1,000) a tonnage clerk with £1.75 weekly rising to £2 and three other clerks receiving from £1.62½–£1.75. By 1842 Freeth was receiving £750 and there were seven clerks receiving £70 to £110pa, together with two apprentices.

There were also staff to supervise the outside works the chief of whom was the superintendent, at first called surveyor of works.

This post was first held on a part-time basis by John Cope but in 1775 it was advertised on a full-time basis for a person having

> a good Knowledge of Figures, of the Value of Materials for Repairs, and of the different prices of Labour; to be acquainted with the Surveying of Land, the making of Embankments and the several other Operations incident to the proper Regulation . . . of a Canal.[48]

A Mr Lawden was appointed and held the post until 1784 when J. Bough was given the post at a salary of £120, 'the £20 as a recompense for keeping a Horse the more expeditiously to proceed on the Companys business'. He died in 1796 and was replaced by Hood at £150. In 1809 when he left the post was divided into two, each receiving the same salary and being responsible for half the works and so it remained.

Under each superintendent was an engineer, at first paid on a weekly basis and obviously of lesser status. By 1811 the salary was £50pa and seems to have remained there.

These can be called the central staff. The remainder were scattered round the various key points in the system and can be broadly considered as clerical or manual. The chief clerical staff were there in charge of wharves. When the canal was first opened the wharf near Friday Street was put in charge of a 'Superintendent' at £50pa, assisted by a wharfinger (£26) with two weighers at 9s per week, two writers at 12s and two watchmen at 6s. The first two posts were later combined as wharfinger at £70pa with an assistant at £30 and, as business increased, a night machine-minder appointed at 12s 6d. The weekly wages seem to have been variable as watchmen sometimes received 10s 6d and 'cheque-clerks' 14s to 21s.

References to staff at other wharves are less detailed, though the wharfingers at Wolverhampton and Fazeley each had an assistant.

The tax returns of 1826 and 1827 (the only ones we have) show that there were eleven or twelve 'collectors', of whom four doubled as lock-keepers and five or six as book-keepers (and whose

MAINTENANCE AND OPERATION 163

salaries ranged from £20 to £50pa) together with three machine clerks (presumably one at each wharf) and four ticket makers (at Darlaston, Riders Green, Tipton and Gospel Oak at 15s–18spw), of whom two or three doubled as lock-keepers. There were also two lock-keeper/book-keepers so that it is clear that the division between manual and clerical labour was far from clear cut! By 1842 the salaries of collectors and lock-keepers totalled £1,577, ranging from £31.20pa at Curdworth to £160pa at Horsley Field.

As far as the manual workers were concerned, the only consistent policy one can find is that of keeping them to a minimum. When the Fazeley Canal was complete an *ad hoc* committee was set up to advise on dismissals, which also appointed Edmund Gooden as general supervisor of manual labour while Houghton advised that 'the whole Line wants & must have a thorough Weeding of all superfluous Hands and Hangers on let us have none but good men & pay those well & we shall find a very small number sufficient'.[49]

This, of course, referred to canal building. In normal times, if any were normal, the main manual work-force was the lock-keepers, who, at first, were paid 10s (50p)pw with a house. By the end of the century they were acting as maintenance staff as well and, as a result, wages were raised, in some cases to 21s a week. Extra gratuities, usually of £5, were paid annually for night work. At one time a discussion took place as to whether it would be useful to appoint more lock-keepers to prevent evasion of regulations. On the advice of Bull and Bough, the engineers, it was decided it would be more useful to appoint an inspector of lock-keepers and Piddock, a lock-keeper, was promoted.

The dual function is clearly seen in decisions taken on the advice of Piddock's son, then 'Walking Surveyor', concerning the Fazeley line in 1825. The two lock-houses at Aston were to have a night and a day man, both carpenters with responsibility for the woodwork of the eleven Aston locks. There were two houses at Minworth, one to be occupied by a carpenter who received 21spw plus 30s a quarter, and a third to be built at the bottom of the lock. Three existing houses at Curdworth plus another were for day lock-keepers, a fifth for a night man and a sixth for 'a good bricklayer'.

The varying numbers employed can be seen from the work of the Accounts Committee. In 1813 there were five permanent bricklayers whose wages ranged from 3s 6d (17½p) to 4s 6d (22½p) a day with a house and eight temporary at 2s (10p) to 3s 6d (17½p). There were nine carpenters at 2s 8d (13½p) to 4s (20p), one stone mason at 27s (£1.35)pw, eight 'agents and labourers' at 21s (£1.05)pw and four 'servers' at 2s (10p) to 2s 6d (12½p) per day. By 1820 this had changed to

> eleven carpenters at 3s 6d–5s (17½p–25p)
> eleven bricklayers at 3s 6d–4s (17½p–20p)
> four stonemasons at 4s–5s 3d (20p–26p)
> five blacksmiths at 3s–4s (15p–20p)
> twenty-seven labourers at 1s 8d–3s (8½p–15p)
> seven occasional men at 3s 4d–4s 6d (16½p–22½p)
> (Including two boatbuilders and two fitters-up).

At the beginning of the next year ten of these were sacked in an economy drive, and a year later there remained three carpenters at 3s 6d (17½p), nine stonemasons at 3s (15p) to 5s 3d (26p), two blacksmiths at 3s (15p) to 4s (20p) and nineteen labourers at 2s (10p) to 4s (20p).

By 1842 the 'Maintenance Division', as it was called, was under control of five inspectors, with salaries ranging from £130 to £180pa. They covered four districts, since two were at that time allocated to the district which included the newly-merged Wyrley & Essington Canal. 'Each Inspector [had] under his charge a number of Carpenters, Blacksmiths, Bricklayers and labourers, proportionate to his District',[50] hired and fired by him and with wages totalling £7,864, which suggests a total of over one hundred. A 'Board of Inspectors' was held every Friday, the Clerk being present, to hear reports and order repairs.

In addition there were enginemen, whose supervisor received £248pa in 1842. In 1820 their wages ranged from 4s 2d (21p) to 5s 6d (27½p) per day with nine assistants receiving 3s 6d (17½p).

They were allowed an extra 4s (20p) per week when they worked Sundays.

There was, of course, pressure for increased wages as prices went up during the French Wars. This was sometimes conceded, but generally resisted, 'temporary allowances' being made annually instead to those the engineer 'considered deserving thereof'; after the war the Accounts Committee recommended 'the propriety of an attempt to reduce the Wages of the Companys Workmen & Labourers in consequence of the reduced price of Provisions'.[51]

The company had no organised insurance scheme like that operated by Boulton & Watt, but *ad hoc* payments were made to 'deserving cases'. Thus a guinea was given to Benjamin Partridge, 'he having had the Misfortune to be hurt in launching a Boat' and 10s 6d (52½p) was paid for the doctor's bill when the engineman at Spon Lane was hurt in an accident. In 1801 a guinea was given to the aged widow of a lock-keeper drowned in a lock 'towards her present exigencies'. Such payments were clearly not a right; their comparative rarity and arbitrary nature—another widow of a drowned lock-keeper received £20—suggests that many in need received nothing. However, there was a tendency for the numbers assisted to increase and for the amounts paid to grow larger. In 1824, for example, the committee called for a report 'of any of the Company's Servants who upon account of Accident or Sickness may be unable to work that [they] may determine what allowance shall be made during their incapacity',[52] and, when Richard Foster, a clerk, resigned after thirteen years because of failing sight, he was given £50. A lock-keeper who retired at the age of 79 after serving the company 54 years was given 10s a week. In 1807 Hood was asked to report what he had done 'towards the establishment of a Club for the assistance of the Comp^{ys} Servants & Workmen when Sick or Lame',[53] but there is no further mention of it.

All in all, however, the impression from a survey of the labour supply of the company, as with many other aspects of its organisation, is of a modern business. There was little sign of scientific management, and none of costing, but there was a clear attempt to achieve efficiency, to eliminate waste and to reduce problems to measurable terms of profit and loss. In this the company was again in advance of its day and environment.

Page 167   (*above*) Parkhead junction above Blowers Green lock on the Dudley Canal, 1955. The viaduct is that of the Oxford, Worcester & Wolverhampton Railway; (*below*) buildings in course of demolition which were built over the side-pounds of the Farmer's Bridge locks

Page 168 (*above*) Toll-office, now demolished, at Wednesfield Stop at the junction of the Bentley Canal with the Wyrley & Essington Canal, 1965; (*below*) Bentley Canal top lock and lock-house, 1965

CHAPTER 8

The Coming of the Railways

As early as 1810 the Birmingham Canal had been disturbed by a plan, devised by William James, for a canal and railway between Walsall and Fazeley, but this was merely a straw in the wind. Twelve more years elapsed before Thomas Moss Tate Esq of Toxteth Park near Liverpool alerted them to 'a combination of Speculators at Liverpool & Manchester with the Iron & Coal Masters in this neighbourhood to promote plans of Carriage by Land with the power of Steam upon Iron Railway'. In reply it was resolved that 'the Committee will neglect no opportunities or endeavours to protect the Company's Interests & Property from innovation or injury'[1]—a resolve that was to be called upon often in the next twenty-five years. As a first step it was agreed to oppose the Liverpool & Manchester Railway Bill, presumably as setting a bad example. Example or no, within a year an attempt was being made to raise a subscription of £50,000 'to establish a Rail Road from the Collieries to Birmingham to supply the Town . . . with Coals at a much cheaper rate than has hitherto been effected' and letters were sent to other canals for support. When the first Liverpool and Birmingham Bill was mooted a Proprietor ('who wishes his name not to be mentioned') gave it as his opinion that it was a judgement on the canals in that 'it originated on the refusal of Canal C[os] to accomodate & encourage the Trade in opposition to the Welch Trade'—though he felt 'the Brm & the G[d] Trunk Cos stand free from censure', one may assume that it was considerations such as this which led soon after to the decision to call in Telford. Anyway the committee decided to oppose the Bill since, 'in case such project should be carried into effect it may tend to the establishment of similar Undertakings in other Districts & directions & deteriorate the Property invested in Canals'.² Other canals were approached, as were landowners on the proposed line of the railway.

The prospectus for the new railway promised to carry goods at 8mph and (probably) passengers at 12mph—'but as no experiments have been made upon a large scale, with a view to establishing the fact, they do not pledge themselves to this.' Direct reference was made to the canals; conveyance would be equally easy 'in periods of frost and drought' and, although developing trade would provide sufficient employment for both canals and railways, the new route would 'create a competition highly advantageous to the public'.³

Correspondence on the subject began immediately in the press. One 'Amicus' suggested that, if the canals would 'wave, for a time, . . . the consideration of income', they could so reduce rates as to force the abandonment of railways 'in a few years', but Dynamics' of London who held both canal and railway shares, felt that

> under the genial influence of the good cheer at the Royal Hotel . . . when delegates from other dirty waters met to cook up the opposition to the Railway, the chairman might have addressed them in the spirit of the adage "Ede, bibe, lude, post mortem nulla voluptas (Cheer up, my friends, eat drink and be merry while your heads are above water—success to monopoly and combination)."
>
> The premium currently offered for rail-road shares . . . and the falling prices of canal property are sufficient evidence of the public estimate of their respective merits.⁴

Opposition was particularly strong to the idea that the canal company had some sort of 'vested rights'.

As F. Finch put it:

> It cannot be denied that if the railroads be established, the individuals who have capital embarked in canals, will lose a part of the profit which they have hitherto derived . . . and I, for one,

will say that they have enjoyed their inordinate profits quite long enough . . . The Public interest is what most needs attention; individuals and companies are sufficiently able to take care of their own. Monopolies are the bane of trade & when once established are difficult to get rid of.[5]

It was the sort of attack the Birmingham Canals had faced before; however justified it may have been, they had survived, and they would do so again.

The petition for the Bill was submitted on 18 February 1825 and its supporters endeavoured to discredit opposition by parodies of petitions:

> That your petitioners have in no instance received more than fifty per cent in dividends . . . quite inadequate as a remuneration for the expence and anxiety they have had in bringing the said useful public works to maturity . . . it must be evident to your Honourable House that such intentions [of the supporters of the railway] are entirely at variance with those of your petitioners as they are completely confined to profit

and law reports:

> The plaintiffs . . . charged the defendants . . . that 'they had wantonly fraudulently and maliciously united' with a view to deprive them of their vested rights; that having more than fifty years ago opened a Canal communication entirely for the public good in the first instance, they have a just claim to receive back annually the sum originally advanced.[6]

The Bill was defeated in that Session, 'upon the alleged ground of the omission of a single Township in the Notices', but reappeared in the next, its promoters taking credit for 'the great alterations and improvements which have been projected in different Canals . . . and in none more striking than in the instance of the Birmingham Canal', which was not only improving its own main line but also promoting a new canal from Wolverhampton to Nantwich, 'upon or near the very line of the proposed Railway, thereby giving a direct negative to the assertion . . . that the present lines of transit are sufficient'.[7] They offered to cut the time from 60 to 15 hours and the cost from £2.25 to £1.50 per ton.

The Birmingham Canal committee sent one of its member to Darlington 'to inspect the state of the Rail Road lately laid down there, and ascertain how far the Operation of Loco Motive Steam Engines answer the purposes . . . held out',[8] and set up a sub-committee to handle its opposition to the Bill. On this occasion also they were successful; the railway company was dissolved on 22 June 1826, but the new canal (the Birmingham & Liverpool Junction) received Parliamentary assent. The supporters of the railway decided to concentrate on a route between Birmingham and Wolverhampton only, in order to 'moderate the long existing grievance' of the excessive charges and profits on the canal but were no more successful in that.

However, the Liverpool and Birmingham Railway eventually gained its Act (in 1833, by which time it had changed its route, and its name to the Grand Junction) in spite of this opposition, as did the London & Birmingham, but the BCN continued to oppose new lines. In 1830 and again in 1835 they were to be found devoting their energies to the fight against the Birmingham, Dudley & Wolverhampton Railway, but signs of a new approach were visible at the latter date when agreement was reached to join the Grand Junction Railway in opposition. As a result of this combined opposition 'together with the manifest indifference of the inhabitants of Dudley and Wolverhampton to the undertaking', it was wound up in November 1836. The Grand Connection (Worcester and Wolverhampton) Railway, however, managed to scrape through in committee notwithstanding, so it was claimed,

> the united efforts of several highly influential though unfriendly landowners, in combination with a wealthy, and of course jealous canal monopoly whose strength was not the less powerful though not formally represented[9]

By this time the 'Little Railway Mania' was dying away and in November 1837 the cashier of the BCN could say: 'As regards the expense for opposing Rail Road Schemes he has only to state, that he hopes, this is the last time such an item will appear in the

Account'.[10] This was not such wishful thinking as it might appear because the attitude of the company had been changing; it was becoming clearer that a *modus vivendi* might be possible.

Signs of this were visible as early as 1830, when a sub-committee was set up to consider the effect only of railways 'on lines parallel to the Birm Canal'. When the Rochdale Canal Company suggested combined opposition to railway Bills they were informed that it was the committee's opinion 'that it would be more expedient for each Canal Company to defend itself upon its independent merits against such Railways as may affect its interests, whereby each Company might be enabled to state a stronger case than by a combined opposition'[11]—an attitude which presumably sprang from the belief that the BCN would do best in such circumstances. In pursuit of this new policy the committee declined to join other canals in the cost of opposing the London & Birmingham Railway and opposition thereafter tended to be on specific points, such as proposed diversions of the canal or the construction of parallel embankments which would interfere with their power to build branches. Clauses were prepared for insertion in the London & Birmingham Railway Bill 'for the prevention of Hindrance and Obstruction to this Canal and for the preservation and protection of the rights, priviledges and authorities of the Company',[12] and dissent was usually registered to any proposal by a railway to cross the canal.

Once the necessary clauses had been agreed, opposition ended and as early as January 1835 the contractor for the Duddesworth viaduct on the Grand Junction Railway was allowed to unload his boat-loads of stone at the nearest point on the canal 'on the Offside of the Canal, and the blocks of Stone raised by pullies therefrom, and then by means of beams to be placed across the Canal, at the height of 12 feet above top water, swing across the Canal and towing path'[13]—a system which would seem to give ample grounds for objection if it were required—and a few months later permission was given to the resident engineer of the London & Birmingham Railway to erect coffer dams at Nova Scotia Gardens. Both railways were charged a mere £5 annually for the privilege of passing under or over the canal and the friendly relationship was shown in 1838 when, the Grand Junction contractor having turned water into the aqueduct over the railway at Darlaston before it was ready, Joseph Locke suggested 'since your Men are probably better acquainted with such Works, if you will put them to do it in their own way I undertake . . . to pay any reasonable Sum'[14] and the matter was settled on the spot.

Once it was clear that railways were there to stay, the question arose as to how their competition could be dealt with. This directed attention immediately to the question of tolls, and consideration was given to this matter as early as 1829, at the instance of the Oxford and Warwick & Napton Canals, but with no result. A request from the same canals and others the next year for consideration to be given to reducing tolls specifically to meet potential railway opposition met with a direct refusal; when a sub-committee was appointed on the subject the danger it was to meet was of competition from seaborne coals at Stourport and Gloucester. At this date there were, in fact, many requests from coalowners and others for reductions of tonnage, all refused. The first break was a decision in July 1831 to allow a drawback on coal passing via Oxford to the Thames, but this remained a rare exception, the committee insisting that partial abatements of tolls were prohibited by the Acts. Moreover, they argued that the company

> having for some time past considered the carrying Trade on Canals best promoted by making Improvements in the several Lines of Navigation, and having in conformity therewith expended a heavy Sum in giving facilities on the Birmingham Canal, ought not in the opinion of the Committee to be required in addition to the great outlay already made, to reduce the rates of Tonnage.[15]

Even the decision of the Grand Junction Canal to reduce tolls on coals going south of Cowley by 2s 4¾d (12p) per ton failed to promote their emulation. In general this remained the company's attitude until 1838; as late as February 1837 legal action was being threatened against the two Warwick Canals to force them to end their drawback on coal entering the Oxford Canal at Napton.

The Grand Junction Railway was opened in January 1838, the London & Birmingham in November and the Derby-Hampton line in August 1840. In June 1838 a letter was received from a Liverpool carrier 'relative to the competition of the Grand Junction Railway in the conveyance of commodities between Birmingham and Liverpool' but no action was taken at that stage. By April 1841 Pickfords were advertising their goods as forwarded by rail and two years later the Horsley Coal Company moved to new premises in Railway Street, Wolverhampton.

The canals were not in a good position to meet this threat. In August 1838 Freeth reported to the committee that the distance by canal from Birmingham to Wolverhampton was now less than by either road or rail and rates had consequently fallen but other canals between Birmingham and London had 'undergone no shortening or improvement whatever, the faulty Levels & excessive Lockage of this Route remaining uncorrected', and the length 23 miles further than by rail. The 'vend' of Staffordshire coal in the south had fallen from 270,181 tons in 1832 to 212,376 in 1837 as a result of the agreement between the Coventry and two Warwick Canals to keep up rates and the Stratford Canal 'exhibited the most marked and unaccountable Apathy' towards suggestions of diverting trade to relieve Farmer's Bridge locks.[16]

In the same month the BCN agreed to attend a meeting of canal companies, called by the Grand Junction Canal, to consider reducing tolls to meet railway competition. This gathering decided to cut tolls and then reversed the decision later in the meeting, preferring to wait until the London & Birmingham's rates were known. Even this precarious unity did not last long. The next month it was discovered that iron was already reaching London 'by other means than Canal', but the committee resolved that 'the Grand Junction Committee are not entitled to call upon this Company for a reduction of Tonnage until they have shortened and improved their own Line and obtained an adequate supply of water'.[17]

Nevertheless, unilateral reductions were made. Tolls on a range of manufactured goods fell from $1\frac{1}{2}$d to 1d per ton/mile in

November, following a similar reduction by the Grand Junction Railway. Revenue fell slightly: 'Notwithstanding the lowering of the rates considerable quantities of light goods are now being, and will probably continue to be, conveyed by railway between Manchester and London and Birm^m and London'.[18] The point was, of course, that 'light goods' were not the life-blood of the Birmingham Canal, who therefore refused to reduce tolls on a comparatively minor item such as wool even when told that the railway rate was so low 'that unless a material reduction be made in the Canal Tolls the conveyance of it by water cannot be retained'. Coal was another matter, and the toll from Farmer's Bridge to Fazeley was halved in October 1840 to meet competition, as was that via Digbeth a year later. Similar reductions followed on other routes, usually confined to coal for the long-distance trade, which was where competition was most severe, but 1s 3d (6p) was cut from the rate between Birmingham and Wolverhampton at the end of 1841 and reductions became general the year after, when the coal and iron trade were entering a general depression. In 1844 a special traffic and tolls subcommittee was set up with power to vary tolls as they saw fit.

These measures had some success in retaining trade, though they obviously reduced revenue per ton/mile, but they were not enough. As early as 1824 Baxendale of Pickfords told John Houghton

> That the Canal Proprietors though in receipt of immense Profits considering themselves secure in their Monopoly had disregarded the Commercial Interests & although rapid Progress had been made in improving Roads & removing public obstructions Canal Cos were dormant . . .
>
> Mr Baxendale stated that since he joined Pickfords concern they have expended upwards of £45,000 in Buildings, Cranes &c to give dispatch to business & is of opinion that a corresponding disposition in Canal Cos would have prevented every attempt at oppositions . . . He is no advocate for the reduction of Rates, if reasonable. He wishes the Canal Proprietors to be able to remove obstructions and promote Dispatch & regularity.[19]

This was a lesson the Birmingham Canal learned well, and they never ceased to bemoan the 'supineness and want of spirit' of the other canals in this respect. In October 1824 they attended a fruitless meeting of canals between Manchester and London 'to consider the improving by every practicable means the present Line of Inland Navigation', and one of the main reasons for wishing to by-pass the Farmer's Bridge locks was that the delays there rendered the other improvements of less value than they could be. Thus the BCN was urged by Freeth to support the London & Birmingham Junction Canal (from near Coventry to the northern Stratford Canal) since it would divert long-distance trade to the route via Worcester Bar even though there would be some losses on the Fazeley traffic. A recommendation that the company support the Bill 'by all the interest they possess' was, however, rejected by the General Assembly.

A renewed, and more ambitious, plan was put forward in 1836, to link the Stratford Canal to the Regent's Canal. This time it was supported, since 'without the outlet such additional Line would give [the BCN] would never reap the full fruit of the great expenditure they had incurred'.[20] It was claimed the new line would save 36 miles and 129 locks, with a 50 per cent saving on tolls. Capital was to be £3,000,000, the promoters stating it as their belief that 'though Railway conveyance may be preferred for passengers and light goods that require dispatch and will bear high rates of transit, the great bulk of the trade of the country will still be carried on through the medium of cheap navigable communications'.[21] Unfortunately the public did not think likewise and the project disappeared without trace in the welter of railway projects.

Nothing daunted, the BCN transferred their support to the Manchester & Birmingham Junction Canal, from the Bridgewater Canal near Altrincham to the Middlewich branch of the Ellesmere & Chester Canal near Middlewich. Unfortunately the project was crippled from the start by having to concede to the Bridgewater Canal the right to charge 3s 8d (18½p) per ton for the 8 miles used of their route and to the Trent & Mersey Canal the right to receive 10½d per ton compensation on all goods entering their line—shortsighted attention to immediate interests which does much to explain the success of the railways. The fate of the Birmingham & Liverpool Junction Canal, keenly supported by the BCN as a northward extension of their improved line, was also a deterrent; in 1838 they had still paid no dividend and their £100 shares stood at £24.

These latter facts perhaps explain why the Birmingham Canal was persistently hostile to the suggestion of a canal to join the BCN near Wolverhampton directly to the Birmingham & Liverpool Junction Canal, even though the water needed would presumably be saved on the Wolverhampton locks. They dissented from it when it was first suggested in 1836 and it was withdrawn, the Staffs & Worcs Canal reducing their compensation tolls from 1s to 4d instead. It was revived five years later and again dissent was registered before it disappeared.

Even as late as May 1844, however, when new canal projects were beginning to look hopeless, a favourable response was given to a deputation of mineowners urging a new line of canal from the Fazeley Canal to the Oxford Canal to avoid the high tolls still charged, by agreement, on the Coventry and Warwick Canals. A survey was ordered and the resulting plan approved. By July the project had its own provisional committee and the BCN offered to lease it on completion for $3\frac{1}{2}$ per cent plus half of the surplus, but that is the last we hear of it.

If routes could not be improved, perhaps speed could, and from around 1830 increased facilities were given to fly-boats. These even began to carry passengers; in 1830 the *Euphrates* packet did the return journey between Wolverhampton and Birmingham each weekday with passengers and parcels, leaving Wolverhampton at 6 am and Birmingham at 5 pm. By 1843 there were two packets each way each day and an extra boat was put on for the Birmingham Music Festival. Fares were 1s 6d ($7\frac{1}{2}$p) 'Chief Cabin' and 1s 2d (6p) Second Cabin. A year earlier there were four in each direction daily. In 1835 fly-boats were given preference over all other boats at the locks between 3 pm and 8 am (provided they were within a hundred yards of the lock)—soon changed to

THE COMING OF THE RAILWAYS 179

FIGURE 8. Advertisement for goods wharf and fly-boats, showing trade in general goods from the BCN

6 pm to 6 am. However, speed could be a problem and eight years later such boats were restricted to one horse because of their 'excessive speed', Pickfords complaining even so of the damage caused by them passing their basin 'as fast as the Horses can Gallop'. Soon afterwards they were given precedence in all circumstances at Tipton locks. The BCN, however, never went as far in this direction as the Birmingham & Liverpool Junction Canal which, by 1844, was advertising steam tug boats with trains of boats twice daily. Experiments had convinced them that the damage to the banks was too great.

In spite of all efforts, however, the revenue and profits of the

Birmingham Canal did not improve; the tendency was towards stagnation of revenue and decline of profits as the figures show:[22]

Half year ending	Revenue £	Profits £	Dividend £
March 1840	61,162	33,991	33,130
Sept 1840	65,579	38,788	36,506
March 1841	63,485	31,797	36,897
Sept 1841	63,160	42,032	37,030
March 1842	62,114	35,274	37,240
Sept 1842	50,444	24,763	37,378
March 1843	60,087	33,929	36,349
Sept 1843	51,358	23,811	36,438
March 1844	60,488	31,305	36,536
Sept 1844	57,334	32,991	36,641
March 1845	62,533	24,427	28,472
Sept 1845	62,507	25,390	28,795

Profits reached a peak, at an annual rate of 120 per cent, in September 1841, but even the previous year they had failed to pay the dividend, and they never did so thereafter. That this was not known to the proprietors is shown by the fact that, nevertheless, £5,000 was spent from revenue on new works in the half-year ending March 1842 and £6,986 in the next. The resulting drain on the cash balance forced the return of £9,000 in the next half-year and the committee recommended that the dividend be cut by £1 but were defeated in the General Assembly by 1,998 votes to 2,266. However, they did persuade the Assembly to agree to the return of all the money made over from revenue for New Works, a total of £28,628. For the rest of the canal's independent existence the dividend, though cut in September 1844, was kept up by drafts on reserves totalling nearly £15,000, the last such call exhausting them but keeping up the essential facade for the negotiations with the railway. Even so the real deficit, as can be seen, was even greater.

The reason for this decline becomes apparent when we look at the tonnage figures.[23] Total tonnage was 373,541 in March 1841, a figure it did not reach again, partly because of a prolonged slump in the local iron trade, until January 1846; in 1843 it fell below 250,000 tons monthly. Within these over all figures a considerable change was taking place:

	March 1841 tons	March 1846 tons
COAL For Birmingham	38,161	40,985
For works in the mining district	102,255	104,900
Total local trade	140,416	145,885
via Worcester Canal	19,909	5,040
via Warwick Canal	17,962	7,701
via Coventry Canal	1,121	201
via Staffs & Worcs Canal	4,617	3,079
via Whittington and Fazeley	1,406	380
Total distant trade	45,015	16,401
TOTAL COAL	185,431	162,286

OTHER LOCAL TRADE

	March 1841 tons	March 1846 tons
Ironstone	39,960	39,839
Lime & Limestone	27,706	21,070
Sand	4,776	5,576
Road materials & manure	9,439	9,906
Bricks	—	6,533
Total	81,881	82,924
General merchandise	106,229	87,478
	373,541	332,688

It is clear that coal, 'the article which constitutes the great staple business of the canal',[24] retained its predominance but that the distant trade in coal (and probably in general merchandise, which is not itemised separately) was being lost. (This is, in large degree, why revenue had not fallen, since it was on the distant trade that the tolls had been cut). In view of the condition of neighbouring canals, the BCN took its successes as renewed proof

> of what can be done by energy and determination, and is well calculated to add to the impression now rapidly gaining ground, that the low price of Canal stock and diversion of Traffic is less to be ascribed to opposing railways, than to the inactivity, want of foresight, and absurd jealousies of the Canal Companies themselves.[25]

Such reiterated statements sound rather self-righteous, but they held a good deal of truth. If all canals had modernised as did the BCN (and many, having been built later when costs were higher, never had the resources to do so) railways would not have ceased to develop, but it is probable that the canals would have kept a far greater proportion of the bulk traffic, and perhaps even paid dividends as good as those of the railways. But they did not, and the Birmingham Canal had to live with the situation; how it could do so, relying on its advantages for the local trade, can be seen from the figures given. They were not slow to take the moral.

The year 1844 saw them opposing the Oxford, Worcester & Wolverhampton Railway. Opposition was, however, becoming more selective and more a matter of political bargains which might involve support for other railways. They agreed to oppose the Birmingham and Shrewsbury Railway, for example, in return for Grand Junction support against the OWWR. When, therefore the Staffs & Worcs Canal invited the BCN 'to confer on the propriety of arranging a Coalition of the Canals in this District in opposition to the projected Lines of the Railway', they eventually decided that 'under all the Circumstances . . . [it is] no longer expedient to carry on any united opposition to the various projected Railways' and, in the event, continued their opposition only to the Dudley and Bescot Railway and the Birmingham and Shrewsbury.[26]

The opposition to the Dudley and Bescot Railway brought the BCN into contact with the London & Birmingham Railway, who were supporting it, and the latter were persuaded to make certain alterations in the line so that it became less objectionable. Following this, it was agreed to build a railway/canal interchange near Birmingham station and, apparently 'out of the blue', discussions began on a 'Union of Interests'. The basis was to be a guaranteed dividend of £4 10s (£4.50) (later raised to £5) on each existing BCN share from the date of opening of the Rushall Canal, any surplus above this to be equally divided between the two companies and the railway nominating an unspecified number of members to the committee of the canal. As the BCN was, at that time, earning only a £3 dividend the offer was generous indeed and it is not clear where it originated. The two companies were to join in building a railway from Birmingham to Wolverhampton with a branch to Dudley, sharing the profits. The canal would drop its opposition to the London, Worcester & South Staffordshire Railway on condition that this would become part of the line of the proposed Birmingham, Dudley & Wolverhampton Railway. This was no sooner suggested than agreed by the Birmingham committee—not surprisingly in view of the terms—and they made plans for an application to Parliament in the next session for a railway along the banks of the canal. A month later the Shrewsbury & Birmingham Railway was added as a third partner in the new railway. By this time plans were going ahead for the 'wharf' at the railway station.

At this stage the Birmingham committee realised that the £5 guarantee was merely to be a first charge on the profits, if any, of the new railway and decided that they would rather have a non-contingent guarantee of £4 from the London & Birmingham itself; surprisingly, the latter agreed immediately. At this stage, the Stourbridge & Birmingham Railway dissolved itself in favour of a branch from the new line and were given £2,000 by the canal for their *'locus standi* and influence' and six or seven acres at the bottom of Queen Street, Wolverhampton, were purchased as a site for a station.

As the final agreement took shape it became clear that the railway wanted considerable control in return for its money and specified that 'the affairs of the Birmingham Canal Comp^y ... be under the control of the London & Birmingham Railway Company in such manner as shall be effectual to secure the interests of the London & Birmingham Railway Company'.[27] More specifically the railway were to nominate five members of the committee and the canal company were neither to convert debt into shares, to spend more than £500 on any new work, to change tolls nor to enter into alliance with any other railway without permission. The working of the canal was to be under the control of a sub-committee of three from each company, the casting vote to be with the railway or canal according as the guarantee was or was not being invoked at the time. It was decided to raise one-quarter of the capital for the new railway from the public and to bring the Dudley Canal into the discussions.

All this did not proceed without opposition, particularly from those associated with the Grand Junction Railway and its subsidiary the South Staffs railway. At a meeting in Birmingham in October 1845 Lord Hatherton, speaking for these interests, declared that 'such a line as the Birmingham & Dudley should be in the hands of an independent company and not in the hands of any party like the Birmingham Canal Company whose interests must be opposed to the increase of railway accommodation throughout the district'.[28] Even so, the project for a Birmingham & Dudley Junction Railway was soon after abandoned and the opposition of the Grand Junction ceased with the merger that formed the London & North Western Railway.

Matters hung fire for a time, since the General Meeting of the London & Birmingham Railway which would confirm the agreement was not until February 1846. Meanwhile £40,000 was borrowed for the Parliamentary deposit on the new railway and negotiations proceeded with the Dudley Canal. This had previously been mooted thirty years before

> But the gentlemen of the Dudley Canal Committee laying great stress upon the prospective value of their Shares by the Great quantities of Coal remaining upon the line of their Canal And the prospective decrease of the value of the Shares of the Birmingham Canal from the immense quantities of Coal already gotten & sent

to Market and the comparative small quantity remaining, this Meeting (which in other respects was perfectly Harmonious) terminated.[29]

Time had dispersed such illusions and the Dudley Canal were now more than willing. There had, in fact, been some more abortive negotiations in 1839 and the matter was raised again in 1843 when a provisional agreement had been reached. The basis was the division of the then existing BCN shares into two, each resulting share to be taken as equal to one Dudley Canal share, and the plan foundered because the Dudley Canal felt that any plan for a merger which did not involve agreement to improve the physical communication between the two canals would give justified ground of complaint to 'the more important mineral proprietors.' Further talks took place a year later on the same basis, the BCN this time agreeing to the proposal about a new tunnel, but the matter was let drop in view of alleged divisions on the Dudley committee (which do not appear in their minutes).

The BCN now had a trump card, however, and discussions were reopened with a suggestion that they should lease the Dudley Canal for 21 years at £4 10s (£4.50) per share with powers to enforce a merger on the basis of equality of shares (since the last negotiations the BCN shares had been split). The Dudley Canal requested a merger and this was agreed, on an equality basis with the £4 guarantee from the railway extended to the Dudley shares, within a fortnight of the commencement of negotiations. Final agreement was delayed while the exact terms of the railway guarantee were clarified but all was settled by mid-November and a month later the Dudley Canal borrowed £4,000 to pay its shares of the Parliamentary deposits. The necessary Bill had an uneventful passage and became law in July 1846, the final committee meeting being held at the end of that month.

The agreement between the Birmingham Canal and the railway was ratified at a Special Assembly in January 1846; after Mr J. Taylor who had 'delicate banking interests' had resigned from the company because of the financial risk, the decision was unanimous. The necessary Act[30] passed uneventfully into law in August. It was agreed to borrow £400,000 for the Birmingham, Dudley & Wolverhampton Railway. A meeting of shareholders in this railway, now called the Birmingham, Wolverhampton & Stour Valley Railway, was held in May when they were assured that 'it was physically impossible that any railway line could be made to accomodate South Staffordshire not in connexion with the Birmingham Canal. The great and important works in the district were on the line of the Birmingham canal'.[31]

Thus the Birmingham Canal Navigations entered the railway era. More than thirty years later the chairman declared that 'the directors had done wisely in placing themselves under the tutelage of the London and North Western Railway instead of leaving themselves to contend against the continually—increasing encroachments of the railways . . . They might rest under the shadow of the £4 per share'.[32] When one remembers that the £4 was guaranteed on a share for which the original purchase price had been £4 7s 6d (£4.37½), and that the original purchasers had once denied that they could ever hope to gain a 10 per cent return, that statement can rest as a fair epitaph on the business acumen of the Birmingham Canal directors during the period of their independent existence.

Notes

NOTES TO CHAPTER 1 (*pages 11-28*)

1. T. S. Ashton, *Iron and Steel in the Industrial Revolution* (1951), p 244.
2. *Journal of the House of Commons* (*JHC*), Vol 30, pp 720-1. (Petition in favour of the Trent and Mersey Canal), quoted C. Hadfield, *The Canals of the West Midlands* (1966), 17.
3. Eg *Aris's Birmingham Gazette* (*Aris*), 14 April 1766. (From John Dean, Wharfinger of Gainsborough, offering swift transport to London.)
4. Ibid.
5. Ibid, 12 January 1767.
6. Staffordshire Record Office (SRO) D 1788/V/718. (Letter of John Ash to Lord Dartmouth, 3 April 1775).
7. *Aris*, 19 January 1767.
8. British Transport Historical Records (BTHR), *Minute Book of the Birmingham Canal* (*1767-71*). (BCN 1/1), Introductory remarks. This recites the benefits expected, as in 'Well wisher's' letter, but significantly omits reference to the profits for the poor.
9. *Aris*, 2 February 1767.
10. For more details of this conflict see: S. R. Broadbridge: 'Public Interest and Monopoly: the Birmingham Canals 1766-72.' *Transport History*, 5 No 3 (1972), 229-42.
11. BTHR, BCN 1/1, loc cit.
12. BTHR, BCN 1/1, 13 November 1767. The members were Drs John Ash and William Small, Henry Carver and Samuel Garbett Esquires, John Kettle, William Bentley, Matthew Boulton, Joseph Wilkinson and William Welch.
13. *Aris*, 30 November 1767. (Letter from 'T.F.'.)
14. Ibid, 7 December 1767, 11 January 1768. (Letter from 'J.D., an alarmed trader'.)
15. A similar suggestion had been lost in the discussions preceding the Bill for the Sankey Brook Navigation.
16. BTHR, BCN 1/1, 13 & 15 January 1768.
17. 8 Geo III, cap 38.
18. *Aris*, 29 February, 14 March, 4 April 1768.
19. BTHR, BCN 1/1, 8 & 9 June 1768. Thus early was made the suggestion of recirculatory pumping engines.
20. *Aris*, 17 October 1768.
21. *Aris*, 23 October 1769, and BTHR, BCN 1/1, 13 October 1769. Boatmen seem to have been scarce, since Garbett was 'requested to write to Mr Gilbert

at the Duke of Bridgewater's to lend the Co. a Boy or two to steer the Boats' (BTHR, BCN 1/1, 15 November 1769).
22. *Warwickshire Journal*, 26 October, 9 November 1769.
23. J. Freeth, *Inland Navigation: an Ode With Songs, calculated for the first Day the Barges arrive at the Wharf* (2 cnd ed 1769) (Birmingham Reference Library 63268).
24. BTHR, BCN 1/1, 1 December 1769.
25. SRO D564/12/5. (Letter from Garbett to Lord Dartmouth, 19 December 1769.)
26. SRO D564/12/5. Dr Ash commented that their shares, to the number of twenty-four, were sold 'for the small premium of £68 each Share' (SRO D564/12/3. (Letter from Ash to Lord Dartmouth, 3 March 1770).) The minutes of the General Assembly record none of this, but only the replacement of Garbett and Turner by Dr Ash and Elias Wallin (BTHR, BCN 1/1, 29 December 1769).
27. *Warwickshire Journal*, 21 December 1769. (Letter from 'Z, a proprietor'.)
28. *BCN Committee Minute Book (1770–2)*, BTHR, BCN 1/2, 11 May 1770.
29. *Aris*, 19 November 1770 (advertisement).
30. Ibid, 26 November. (Notice of a meeting in West Bromwich), 3 & 24 December 1770, 21 January 1771.
31. *JHC*, Vol 33, 31 January 1771.
32. SRO D564/12/3. (Letter from Colmore to Canal Committee, 23 December 1769.)
33. 11 Geo III, cap 67.
34. SRO D564/12/3. (Letter from Ash to Lord Dartmouth, 30 June 1771.)
35. Ibid. (Copy of letter from Colmore to Ash, 17 July 1771.)
36. *Order Book of the S & W Canal (1776–85)* (BTHR, STW 1/1), 11 January 1770.
37. BTHR, BCN 1/1, 29 February 1770.
38. BTHR, STW 1/1, 20 February 1770.
39. BTHR, BCN 1/2, 16 August 1770. (This followed a request from 'the W-hampton Cttee'); *BCN Assembly Minute Book (1770–6)* (BCN 1/40), 28 September 1770.
40. *JHC*, Vol 33, 31 January 1771. The original Act gave the S & W Canal only powers to build and be reimbursed; they required powers to raise the money in advance.
41. SRO D564/12/5. (Letter from Sir Edward Lyttleton to Lord Dartmouth.)
42. BTHR, BCN 1/2, 10 and 12 April 1771.
43. Ibid, 18 May 1772. The reference to teeth and pinions shows that the paddle gear must have been much as at present.
44. Ibid, 18 May, 13 June 1772.
45. BTHR, BCN 1/40, 27 September 1772.

NOTES TO CHAPTER 2 (*pages 29–45*)

1. *Aris*, 13 March 1775; SRO, D1778/V/718. (Ash to Lord Dartmouth, 4 March 1775.)
2. 16 Geo III, c 28 (Stourbridge Canal), and 16 Geo III, c 66 (Dudley Canal).
3. *Dudley Canal Assembly Minute Book* (1776–45), (BTHR, DDC 1/2), 2 July 1778.
4. Ibid, 7 October 1776, 21 April 1777, 23 March 1777.
5. Ibid, 9 February 1784.
6. *BCN Committee Minute Book* (1784–8) (BTHR, BCN 1/5), 15 January 1785.

7. *BCN Assembly Minute Book (1771–87)* (BTHR, BCN 1/41), 25 March, 15 April 1785.
8. *JHC*, Vol 40, 27 April 1785.
9. *Aris*, 9 May 1785.
10. 25 Geo III, c 87.
11. *Aris*, 29 August 1785.
12. For more details on Pinkerton see below and S. R. Broadbridge, 'John Pinkerton and the Birmingham Canals', *Transport History*, 4 No 1 (1971), pp 33–49.
13. *Dudley Canal Committee Minute Book (1785–93)* (BTHR, DDC 1/3), 29 August, 8 September 1786, 8 & 23 January 1787.
14. J. Pinkerton, *Abstract of the Cause* . . . (1801) (Birmingham Reference Library 3119), p 232; DDC 1/3, 3 & 20 July 1787.
15. 30 Geo III, c 60.
16. *BCN Committee Minute Book (1793–9)* (BTHR, BCN 1/7A), 12 September 1794.
17. *Dudley Canal Committee Minute Book (1793–9)* (BTHR, DDC 1/4), 1 October 1779 *Dudley Canal Committee Minute Book (1800–7)* (DDC 1/5), 23 February, 29 October 1792.
18. *Aris*, 3 September, 1 October 1781.
19. SRO D1778/V/622 (Draft pamphlet); *House of Commons Journal*, Vol 38, 18 February 1782.
20. BTHR, BCN 1/41, 3 January 1783, *House of Commons Journal*, Vol 39, 31 January 1783.
21. W. Hutton, *A History of Birmingham* (1795), p 409.
22. *The Case of the Proprietors of the Birmingham Canal* (1783) (Birmingham Reference Library 660153).
23. *Short Reasons why the Bill now depending in Parliament . . . should not pass into a Law* (1783) (Birmingham Reference Library 660153).
24. Anon, *Navigation: a mock heroic on the Present Contest* (1783) (Birmingham Reference Library 78736).
25. Hutton, loc cit.
26. 23 Geo III, c 92.
27. 24 Geo III, c 4.
28. BTHR, BCN 1/7A, 6 & 20 June 1794.
29. 25 Geo III, c 97.
30. *BCN Committee Minute Book (1775–84)* (BTHR, BCN 1/4), 23 April 1784; BCN 1/5, 29 October 1784.
31. BTHR, BCN 1/5, 5 April, 19 May 1786.
32. Ibid, 25 & 30 August 1786.
33. BTHR, BCN 1/5, 12 & 26 January 1787.
34. Pinkerton, op cit, p 230. According to Pinkerton, Bough said, 'Damn it, I knew I was three feet wrong, but I'd not think it had been as much as it is.' (Pinkerton, p 234.)
35. Pinkerton, pp 413–14. (Letter of 26 April 1787.)
36. Pinkerton, op cit, pp 8–9. (Evidence of Lee, the Company's solicitor.)
37. Ibid, pp 17, 36–8. (Evidence of William Hodgkiss, brick layer.)
38. *BCN Committee Minute Book (1788–93)* (BTHR, BCN 1/6), 4 & 18 October, 26 December 1788.
39. *BCN Committee Minute Book (1822–9)* (BTHR, BCN 1/11), 26 September 1823.
40. Pinkerton, op cit, xxv; *BCN General Assembly Minute Book 1787–1815* (BTHR BCN 1/42), 1 October 1802.

NOTES TO CHAPTER 3 (*pages 46-73*)

1. BTHR, STW 1/1, 31 October 1785; BCN 1/5, 3 March 1786.
2. *Aris*, 2 January 1786.
3. 31 Geo III, c 59.
4. BTHR, BCN 1/6, 27 July 1792.
5. *Case in support of a Bill for making a Canal from the Stratford-upon-Avon Canal ... to the Warwick and Birmingham Canal* (1795), quoted in: C. Hadfield and J. Norris, *Waterways to Stratford* (1962), 76.
6. BTHR, BCN 1/7A, 7 February 1794.
7. *Aris*, 16 & 23 December 1799.
8. BTHR, DDC 1/2, 3 September 1792; DDC 1/3, 5 September 1792.
9. *Aris*, 7 January 1793. (Letter from 'An Inhabitant'.)
10. *Minutes of the [BCN] London Committee (1793)* (BTHR, BCN 1/130), 6, 9, 11 & 16 February 1793.
11. BTHR, BCN 1/130, 23 February 1793.
12. 33 Geo III, c 121.
13. *Aris*, 24 June 1793.
14. BTHR, DDC 1/4, 19 January 1796.
15. Ibid, 24 May 1796.
16. *Aris*, 8 January 1798.
17. *Dudley Canal Committee Minute Book (1807-13)* (BTHR, DDC 1/6), 9 October 1810.
18. BTHR, DDC 1/5, 4 March 1800.
19. Ibid, 22 June, 22 July 1800.
20. Ibid, 23 September 1800.
21. Ibid, 3 March 1801, 19 April 1802.
22. BTHR, DDC 1/6, 9 October 1810; DDC 1/2, 7 September 1812.
23. BTHR, DDC 1/6, 3 August 1804.
24. BTHR, DDC 1/5, 16 October 1804.
25. *Dudley Canal Committee Minute Book (1831-46)* (BTHR, DDC 1/9), 11 June, 20 August 1839.
26. DDC 1/9, 8 December 1840, 31 October 1843, 14 January 1845.
27. BTHR, BCN 1/6, 26 August, 30 December 1791, 13 January 1792. For the Wyrley Canal cf C. J. Gibson, 'The Wyrley and Essington Canal,' *Lichfield Archaeological and Historical Society Transactions*, Vol I (1959/60).
28. BTHR, BCN 1/6, 16 March 1792.
29. 32 Geo III, c 81. The Act contained no clause about the junction point but the junction was built as previously agreed. (The sections of the Act are not numbered.)
30. J. Priestley, *Navigable Canals etc.* (1830), p 742.
31. BTHR, BCN 1/7A, 13 September 1794.
32. Ibid, 29 April, 26 August 1796, 6 April 1798.
33. 34 Geo III, c 25. (The sections in this Act, too, are not numbered.)
34. BTHR, *Wyrley and Essington Canal Assembly Minute Book (1792-1840)* (WEC 1/1), 10 May, 10 November 1794.
35. BTHR, WEC 1/1, 30 June 1796.
36. Ibid, 10 November 1797, 10 May 1798.
37. BTHR, WEC 1/1, 7 July 1800, 10 May 1803.
38. Ibid, 12 May 1797; *W & E Canal Committee Memoranda (1797-1803)* (WEC 1/2), 7 & 27 July 1797, 10 November 1803.

NOTES   191

39. Ibid, 11 June [1801] (Memorandum).
40. *Aris*, 10 June 1799. When the reservoir was rebuilt it was faced in stone (WEC 1/2, 3 November 1800).
41. WEC 1/1, 10 May 1799; Vernon's private branch rose twenty-four feet via four locks; it was abandoned in 1829 (Cary, op cit, pp 38-9).
42. BTHR, WEC 1/2, 4 November 1799.
43. Ibid, 27 January 1801.
44. Ibid, 15 August 1803.
45. *BCN Committee Minute Book (1815-22)* (BTHR, BCN 1/10), 8 September 1820.
46. BTHR, WEC 1/1, 11 November 1822.
47. *BCN Memorandum Book (1819-25)* (BTHR, BCN 4/374), 6 January 1824.
48. BTHR, WEC 1/1, 10 May 1825.
49. *Aris*, 28 November 1825.
50. BTHR, BCN 1/42, 5 March 1839.
51. 2 & 3 Vic, c 61.
52. 3 Vic, c 34.
53. *BCN Committee Minute Book (1838-44)* (BTHR, BCN 1/13), 23 April 1841.

NOTES TO CHAPTER 4 (*pages 74-97*)

1. For more detailed consideration of the problems of water supply see Volume III of this work. Cf also S. R. Broadbridge, 'Water Supply on the Birmingham Canals 1767-1830', *Industrial Archaeology*, 10, 3 (1973), pp 279-303.
2. *Report of John Smeaton . . . at a meeting held at the Navigation Office at Birmingham the 9th & 10th October 1782* (MS Copy in Birmingham Central Reference Library 593899).
3. BTHR, BCN 1/4, 23 August 1776.
4. The cost would normally be for materials and their erection only, Boulton & Watt charging a premium thereafter on the basis of coal saved, but there is no record of the payment of such premiums, while the accounts include an item 'Licence for finishing first engine £351-6-4', with another of £210 for the second, which may be lump sums in lieu.
5. BCN, Abstract of Accounts (1775-95) (BCN 4/364), 4 September 1779, 4 March 1780.
6. BTHR, BCN 1/7A, 10 February, 24 March 1797. This was the famous 'Ten Yard Coal' so that the pillars would be thirty feet high.
7. BTHR, *BCN Committee Minute Book (1799-1805)* (BCN 1/7B), 20 August 1802.
8. Ibid, 23-4 August 1804.
9. Ibid, 14 December 1804.
10. BTHR, BCN 1/10, 22 June, 18 August, 1 September 1815.
11. BTHR, *BCN Committee Minute Book (1805-10)* (BCN 1/8), 1 April, 13 May 1808.
12. Ibid, 27 May 1808.
13. [*BCN*] *Select Committee Minutes (1812-22)* (BTHR, BCN 1/48) (Engine Committee), 2 August 1813.
14. BTHR, BCN 1/6, 5 December 1788.
15. BTHR, BCN 1/11, 25 July 1823.
16. *Reports to [BCN] Committees (1823-57)* (BTHR, BCN 1/98), 30 March, 3 August 1827.
17. J. Cary, *Inland Navigation* (1795), 37.

18. BTHR, BCN 1/6, 27 September 1786; BCN 1/41, 29 September 1786. An attempt was made, unsuccessfully, to reverse the decision at the next General Assembly (Ibid, 30 March 1787).
19. BTHR, BCN 1/41, 26 June 1789.
20. *Aris*, 22 June 1789.
21. BTHR, BCN 1/8, 24 March 1809.
22. BTHR, BCN 1/6, 18 September 1790. At the same time a small extension was planned to link the Broadwaters engine with the canal.
23. Ibid, 12 September, 26 October 1792. The third extension was Oldbury/Netherton, the fate of which has already been described.
24. *Swinney's*, 21 February 1793.
25. *Aris*, 4 February 1793.
26. *House of Commons Journal*, Vol 44, 4 March 1793.
27. *BCN Letter Book (1793–1804)* (BTHR, BCN 4/371B). (Letters from Houghton to William Wheeler), 31 December 1793.
28. 34 Geo III, c 87. The Act provided for a reduction on compensation tolls from the Dudley Canal by 6d when the Bloomfield/Deepfield section was opened—perhaps one reason why it was so long in construction.
29. *Aris*, 1 July 1799.
30. BTHR, BCN 1/7B, 9 August 1799. If this was the geometrical lock that Whitmore and Norton put to the Somersetshire Coal Canal about this time, it seems to have been some kind of vertical lift. See Kenneth R. Clew, *The Somersetshire Coal Canal and Railways*, 1970, pp 43 ff.
31. Ibid, 20 February, 6 March 1801.
32. BTHR, BCN 1/8, 12 June 1807.
33. *BCN Committee Minute Book (1811–15)* (BTHR, BCN 1/9), 29 May 1812.
34. BTHR, BCN 1/8, 13 August 1807.
35. BTHR, BCN 1/10, 30 August 1816.
36. 46 Geo III, c 92.
37. 51 Geo III, c 105.
38. BTHR, BCN 1/9, 24 June 1814.
39. Ibid, 26 July 1811.
40. *House of Commons Journal*, Vol 61, 2 April 1806.
41. Ibid, 27 June 1806.
42. BTHR, BCN 1/8, 12 January 1810.
43. BTHR, BCN 1/9, 15 April, 10 & 24 June 1814.
44. Ibid, 14 October 1814
45. Ibid, 17 February 1815.
46. 55 Geo III, c 40.

NOTES TO CHAPTER 5 (*pages* 98–119)

1. BTHR, BCN 1/10, 4 May 1821.
2. BTHR, BCN 1/11, 26 July 1822.
3. Ibid, 11 July 1823.
4. Ibid, 19 March, 2 April 1824.
5. J. Rickman (ed), *The Life of Thomas Telford Civil Engineer, written by himself* (1838), p 82.
6. J. Rickman, op cit, p 83.
7. BCN General Assembly Minute Book (1816–46) (BTHR, BCN 1/43), 25 March 1825.

8. BTHR, BCN 1/11, 23 December 1825.
9. Ibid, 6 January, 3 February 1826.
10. [*BCN*] *Repairs Committee Minute Book (1823–57)* (BTHR, BCN 1/47) (Accounts Committee), 10, 18 & 26 March 1826.
11. BTHR, BCN 1/11, 25 March 1826.
12. Rickman, op cit, p 84.
13. BTHR, BCN 1/11, 25 March 1826.
14. Ibid, 10 June 1826.
15. BTHR, BCN 1/98. (No date, apparently 1833.)
16. BTHR, BCN 1/11, 5 January, 22 June 1827.
17. Ibid, 14 September 1827.
18. Ibid, 28 September 1827.
19. Ibid, 19 June 1829.
20. *BCN Committee Minute Book (1830–8)* (BTHR, BCN 1/12), 29 January 1830; *British Almanac*, 1830, quoted C. Hadfield, *The Canals of the West Midlands* (1966), p 87. Cf also *Wolverhampton Chronicle*, 23 December 1829.
21. BTHR, BCN 1/12, 26 December 1831, 24 February 1832.
22. Ibid, 6 April 1832.
23. BTHR, BCN 1/98, 12 November 1834 (Report by J. Freeth), BCN 1/12, 11 July, 5 September 1834.
24. This later became involved with plans of the Stourbridge Canal to extend to Bloomfield on the BCN, first mooted in 1836 when a company was floated for that purpose (*Wolverhampton Chronicle*, 9 November 1836). The BCN decided to support, given suitable water guarantees (BCN 1/12, 30 September 1836) but, not surprisingly, the Dudley Canal opposed (DDC 1/9, 17 May 1836). The BCN then planned to build the link itself (BCN 1/12, 28 October 1836) but, when the new canal failed to raise the necessary money, becoming merely the Stourbridge Extension Canal, the idea was dropped (ibid, 27 October 1837). A revived plan to connect the Stourbridge Extension with the BCN had a brief life in 1840 but collapsed owing to lack of support (*Wolverhampton Chronicle*, 25 November 1840).
25. 5 Will IV, c 34.
26. BTHR, BCN 1/12, 30 September, 28 October 1836.
27. BTHR, BCN 1/42, 11 May 1838; Rickman, op cit, pp 86.
28. BTHR, BCN 1/12, 29 July 1838.
29. BTHR, BCN 1/12, 12 May 1837.
30. BTHR, BCN 1/13, 28 September 1838.
31. BTHR, BCN 1/13, 28 June 1839.
32. 2 & 3 Vic, c 61.
33. BTHR, BCN 1/13, 8 November 1839.
34. Ibid, 20 January 1840.
35. 3 Vic, c 56.
36. BTHR, BCN 1/13, 26 February 1841.
37. Ibid, 25 October 1842. There had been complaints that the paddles to the Walsall locks were exceedingly stiff and hard to work.
38. Ibid, 25 November 1842.
39. 7 Vic, c 11.
40. BTHR, BCN 1/13, 31 May 1844. The two Warwick Canals and the Coventry Canal had raised their tolls by a cartel agreement in 1833 but were forced to lower them by public pressure in 1841. The agreement was, however, revived and the tolls increased when the Tame Valley line was opened (BCN 1/42, 29 November 1844).

41. BTHR, BCN 1/42, 11 May 1837.
42. Ibid, 8 November 1839.
43. BTHR, BCN 1/13, 13 November 1840, 25 June 1841.

NOTES TO CHAPTER 6 (*pages 120–143*)

1. BTHR, BCN 1/12, 7 May, 4 June 1830. By 1844 T. Eyre Lee was clerk to the Birmingham & Liverpool Junction Canal (*Wolverhampton Chronicle*, 8 May 1844).
2. For example, until late in the Napoleonic Wars, committee members were never to be found amongst those who voted 'loyal addresses', contributed towards voluntary funds for defence against revolutionary France or formed Yeomanry regiments. They included, however, persons to the fore amongst those who opposed slavery, agitated on commercial issues and favoured various liberal reforms. It is, perhaps, significant that the houses of three of them were destroyed in the Priestley riots. The Galtons and Lloyds were both members of the Society of Friends.
3. At first there were three proprietors from Birmingham and one from Wolverhampton. After the Tunnel Act there were twenty-one proprietors from Birmingham, of whom seven served at some time on the Committee of the BCN. (John Francis (3 shares), Harry Hunt (5), Michael Lakin (1), Ben May (4), Sam Pemberton (1), John Richards (2), William Russell (1).)
4. Five major committee members were well-known as coal-owners. Lord Dudley's family held at least sixteen of the original sixty-five shares and the Foleys seven.
5. *An Address to the Public on the new intended Canal from Stourbridge to Worcester* (SRO D260/M/E/430/29). In spite of small dividends the company often helped local collieries—eg by the gift of a new boiler to Messrs Hawkes and Badley (committee members) or a donation to them of £250 for a new engine when they complained of leakage from the tunnel. (BTHR DDC 1/3, 29 December 1792, 2 July 1793.)
6. BTHR, BCN 1/9, 26 February 1813. This followed the setting up of a Repairs Committee in 1812 (ibid, 27 November 1812). A sinking fund had been set up in 1809, investing its funds in government securities (BCN 1/8, 1 December 1809).
7. BTHR 1/48. A typical entry runs: 'It appearing that Mr Hodgkinson has ordered castings for Locks from the Eagle Foundry for which twelve shillings per Cwt is charged although they may be procured elsewhere at 6/6 or 7/- per Cwt it is recommended that he be directed to order no more of them from the Eagle Foundry' (ibid, 27 August 1813).
8. BTHR, BCN 1/43, 27 March 1818.
9. BTHR, BCN 1/48, 12 September, 16 October 1821.
10. Information re dividends from the Assembly Minute Books, BTHR, BCN 1/40–43, and re share prices from Receipts and Expenditure Book, BCN 4/374. It is to be noted that the number of shares, originally 500 of a face value of £140, was doubled by dividing each into two in 1811 and again in 1820, 1823, 1836 and 1840. In the graph all dividends and prices are related to the original undivided shares. Voting rights went only to those who possessed the equivalent of one half of an original share. (58 Geo III, c 19 (1818) Sect. XII). Between 1804 and 1815 Property Tax, which in the end averaged $11\frac{1}{2}$ per cent pa for each share, was paid by the Company for shareholders.

NOTES 195

11. Staffs & Worcs Canal Committee Order Book (BTHR, STW 1/1, 19 December, 1776).
12. *Wolverhampton Chronicle*, 3 December 1845.
13. BTHR, BCN 1/7B, 28 December 1804.
14. BTHR, BCN 1/9, 29 May 1812.
15. BTHR, BCN 1/10, 17 January 1817.
16. *BCN Letter Book (1786–93)* (BTHR, BCN 4/371A), (Houghton to Messrs Orpwood and Leal, Oxford), 16 September 1795: (Houghton to Lord Dartmouth), 30 June 1797.
17. BTHR, BCN 1/13, 16 December 1842.
18. BTHR, BCN 1/7A, 25 October 1793.
19. BTHR, 4/371A. (Circular letter to other Canal Companies), 22 May 1798.
20. BTHR, BCN 1/7B, 11 & 22 January 1805.
21. BTHR, BCN 1/10, 31 July 1818.
22. BTHR, BCN 1/1, 20 October 1769 (General Assembly). This is a 'mark up' of about 6 per cent.
23. SRO D 564/12/3. (Ash to Lord Dartmouth), 3 February 1770. Ash felt that this trade 'may possibly expire in very few years. The Number of private Traders, may soon render, any such association unnecessary: they will be too numerous to enter into destructive Combinations & the Company's Interest must depend on the increase of Tonnage' (ibid, 12 February 1770).
24. BTHR, BCN 1/1, 16 January 1770 (General Assembly).
25. BTHR, BCN 1/40 (Committee for the Local Trade), 5 May 1772.
26. *Aris*, 21 May 1770.
27. BTHR, BCN 1/40, 29 October 1770, 11 January 1772.
28. *Aris*, 3 November 1775.
29. The debt (arising from his failure to provide sureties) was for £400. It was finally liquidated for £567-17-0 capital and interest in 1822! By that time the original deed had been lost so the Company had to enter into an indemnification against any further claim (BCN 1/10, 17 May 1822).
30. J. Bisset: *A Ramble of the Gods round Birmingham* (1800).
31. *Aris*, 15 October 1824.

NOTES TO CHAPTER 7 (*pages* 144–166)

1. BTHR, BCN 1/43, 29 March 1816.
2. BTHR, BCN 1/10, 14 July 1820.
3. BTHR, BCN 1/7A, 18 October 1798.
4. BTHR, BCN 1/10, 23 February 1821.
5. The cost of the water from the Company's engines varied in 1808 from 4¾d per lock (Smethwick) to 6d (Ocker Hill) (BCN 1/8, 15 April 1808).
6. BTHR, BCN 1/10, 18 December 1818.
7. BTHR, BCN 4/374, 16 July 1819.
8. BTHR, BCN 1/11, 23 August 1822. The fall of the Warwick locks was 7ft, those on the BCN 6ft, but the former's engine had an 8ft stroke and 30in cylinder, that of the BCN 6½ft and 26in.
9. BTHR, BCN 4/371A (Houghton to S & W Canal), 9 September 1796.
10. Ibid (Houghton to S & W Canal), 24 September 1796.
11. This example is from *Wolverhampton Chronicle*, 13 May 1840.
12. BTHR, BCN 1/6, 25 August 1788.
13. BTHR, BCN 1/7B, 5 February 1802, 10 February 1804.

14. Ibid, 6 April 1804.
15. BTHR, BCN 1/10, 9 October 1818, 29 January 1819.
16. BTHR, BCN 1/11, 30 April 1824.
17. BTHR, BCN 1/8, 5 April; BCN 1/9, 23 May 1806.
18. BTHR, BCN 1/9, 7 July 1814.
19. BTHR, BCN 1/7A, 10 August 1798; BCN 1/7B, 25 September 1801.
20. BTHR, BCN 1/7B, 5 November 1802.
21. Ibid, 30 November 1804.
22. BTHR, BCN 1/8, 20 October 1809.
23. BTHR, BCN 1/10, 8 March 1822.
24. *Aris*, 18 February 1799.
25. J. Wilkins in J. Pinkerton, *Abstract of the Cause* . . . , p 213. BTHR, BCN 1/11, 20 October 1824.
26. *Aris*, 2 May 1774.
27. J. Bisset, *A Ramble of the Gods* (Note).
28. J. Hutton, *A History of Birmingham* (1795), p 404.
29. *Aris*, 30 July 1787. Wilkinson's first cast-iron boat was launched the next year, at Willey (ibid, 3 April 1788).
30. BTHR, BCN 1/10, 29 March 1816.
31. *Aris*, 28 March, 17 January 1774.
32. *Aris*, 31 August, 3 May 1778, 28 August 1780.
33. BTHR, BCN 1/7A, 2 November 1798.
34. BTHR, BCN 4/374, 4 August 1819.
35. BTHR, BCN, 1/7B, 29 June 1804.
36. BTHR, BCN 1/7B, 5 November 1802.
37. Ibid, 29 September 1804.
38. BTHR, BCN 4/374, 15 March 1821; BCN 1/11, 26 September 1822.
39. BTHR, BCN 1/10, 3 December 1819.
40. BTHR, WEC 1/1, 11 May 1795.
41. Ibid.
42. BTHR, BCN 1/1, 18 May 1770.
43. BTHR, BCN 4/371B, 30 June 1795 (John Houghton to John Woodcock, Coventry Canal).
44. BTHR, BCN 1/9, 9 December 1814; *Aris*, 9 June 1788, 18 May 1789 and passim.
45. BCN 4/371B, 15 June 1798 (Houghton to Pickfords), 20 February 1790 (Houghton to Leech, the steerer's employer). These examples are typical of very many throughout our period.
46. BTHR, BCN 1/10, 8 December 1815; BCN 1/8, 18 May 1810.
47. *Aris*, 28 December 1789.
48. *Aris*, 24 July 1775.
49. BTHR, BCN 4/371A, 20 June 1791 (Houghton to Bough, one of the engineers).
50. BTHR, BCN 1/13, 16 December 1842.
51. BTHR, BCN 1/48, 22 January 1816.
52. BTHR, BCN 1/11, 6 February 1824.
53. BTHR, BCN 1/8, 3 January 1807.

NOTES TO CHAPTER 8 (*pages 169–186*)

1. BTHR, BCN 1/11, 26 July 1822.
2. Ibid, 13 June 1823; BCN 4/374, 9 April 1824; BCN 1/11, 30 April 1824.

NOTES

3. *Aris*, 13 September 1824.
4. Ibid, 20 September, 6 December 1824.
5. Ibid, 13 December 1824.
6. *Aris*, 21 & 14 March 1825.
7. Ibid, 6 March 1826.
8. BTHR, BCN 1/11, 6 January 1826.
9. *Wolverhampton Chronicle*, 9 November 1836, 26 April 1837.
10. BTHR, BCN 1/42, 10 November 1837.
11. BTHR.
12. BTHR, BCN 1/42, 25 March 1831.
13. BTHR, BCN 1/12, 23 January 1835.
14. Ibid, 28 August 1838.
15. BTHR, BCN 1/12, 6 April 1832.
16. BTHR, BCN 1/13, 28 August 1838.
17. Ibid, 28 September 1838.
18. Ibid, 9 November 1838.
19. BTHR, BCN 4/374, 17 November 1824.
20. BTHR, BCN 1/12, 25 March 1836.
21. *Wolverhampton Chronicle*, 23 & 30 March 1836.
22. Figures from half-yearly reports to the committee, which commenced in 1840. The figures are not therefore necessarily the same as those in the *Abstract of Accounts*. It should be noted that a considerable proportion of income was owed on credit at any one time: in March 1840 £29,103 was so owed and this had grown to £35,970 in September 1845, when the treasurer had to advance the company £11,151 in order to pay current expenses, including dividend.
23. Tonnage figures, in detail, were reported to the committee monthly from 1841.
24. BTHR, BCN 1/13, 26 March 1841.
25. BTHR, BCN 1/42, 14 May 1841.
26. *BTHR Staffordshire and Worcestershire Canal Committee Minute Book (1836-51)* (BTHR, STW 1/6), 12 & 30 December 1844; *BCN Committee Minute Book (1844-50)*, BCN 1/14, 13 December 1844.
27. BTHR, BCN 1/14, 19 August 1845.
28. *Wolverhampton Chronicle*, 29 October 1845.
29. BTHR, BCN 1/9, 29 October 1813.
30. 9 & 10 Vic, c 244.
31. *Wolverhampton Chronicle*, 27 May 1846.
32. *BCN General Assembly Minute Book* (BTHR, BCN 1/45), 22 February 1878.

Acknowledgements

IT will be obvious that without the help of the staff of several libraries, this book would have been impossible. My thanks therefore go to the Librarians and staffs at the British Transport Historical Records (especially since it became part of the Public Record Office), the Staffordshire County Record Office and William Salt Library, and Birmingham and Wolverhampton Public Libraries. The staffs of the North Staffs Polytechnic Library and the National Central Library worked wonders in tracing a copy of *Industry Illustrated* and Mr J. Watson of Greenwich Local History Library took the necessary photographs.

Mr Dennis Kitley gave invaluable help with the photography and my wife shared the burden of searching through newspapers and directories, besides reading and criticising each chapter as it was written. Above all, without Mrs Joan Neal's painstaking unravelling of my writing and its transformation into readable typescript this book would not have seen the light of day.

I should like to thank Mr Philip Weaver for providing the pictures on p 67 (*below*), p 149, p 167 (*above*) and p 168. All other photographs are by the author.

Figure 3 is taken from the Wolverhampton Directory, 1827, and Fig 8 from the 1837 issue. Figs 4 and 5 are from Anon: *Industry Illustrated* (a life of Jackson, the contractor for the Tame Valley Canal), 1865.

Index

Note: Financial matters concerning individual canals will be found under the general headings: Finance; Profits and Dividends; Tolls.

Accidents: Bordesley Embankment (1799), 152; Cannock Heath Reservoir (1799), 66; Drayton Mill (1795), 152; River Tame Aqueduct (1789), 45
Acts of Parliament: Birmingham Canal Navigation(s) (1768), 16; (1771), 23; (1785), 42; (1794), 88; (1806), 92; (1811), 93; (1835), 108; (1839: Walsall Extension), 73; (1840: Merger with Wyrley & Essington), 73; (1844), 116; (1846: Merger with Dudley), 185; (1846: Merger with LNWR), 185–6; Birmingham & Fazeley Canal (1783), 40–1; Dudley Canal (1776), 30; (1785), 34–5; (1790), 36; (1793: Selly Oak), 53–4; Stourbridge Canal (1776), 30; Tame Valley Canal (1839), 111–12; (1840), 113; Warwick & Birmingham Canal (1793), 48; Warwick & Napton Canal (1794), 48; Worcester & Birmingham Canal (1791), 47; Worcester Bar (1815), 94, 95–7; Wyrley & Essington Canal (1792), 62; (1794), 63
Anson Branch, 106, 113

Aqueducts: Leasowes (Dudley Canal), 55; Puppy Green (BCN), 106; Steward (BCN), 105; Tame (Coventry Canal), 45
Ash, Dr John, 21n, 24, 122, 140
Aston, Richard, 35

Bagnall (coalowner): undermining canal, 76
Bank protection, 93
Banks, Read and Dumaresq (coalowners): undermining canal, 75
Barker, William (ironmaster), 135
Bentley, William, 14, 17–18, 21–2, 122; dispute with Garbett, 20
Bentley Branch (BCN Wyrley), 104, 113–16
Beswick, John (contractor), 25, 31, 42
Birmingham (geography), 11
Birmingham Canal Navigation(s): branches—*see* under name of branch; Committee, 14, 17; and control, 120–4; construction, 17–19, 23–4, 26–8; cost estimates, 13–14; maintenance, 144–53; mergers (with Dudley Canal), 184–5; (with London &

199

INDEX

Birmingham Canal cont.
   Birmingham Rly), 182–6; (with Wyrley & Essington Canal), 70–3; minor extensions, 90–3; and monopoly, 21–2; proprietors, 13, 120–1; and public interest, 14–16, 29–30, 38–9, 170–1; and railways, 182; route, 14, 17–18, 24; sub-committees, 126–7; terminus disputes, 19, 22–4; water—*see* Pumping Engines, Reservoirs, Water Supply
Birmingham & Fazeley Canal: struggle for, 38–40; construction, 40–5
Birmingham Heath Branch (BCN), 89
Birmingham & Liverpool Junction Canal, 171–2, 178, 179
Birmingham & Netherton Canal (proposed), 51–3
Birmingham & Warwick Junction (Bordesley) Canal, 112–13
Bloomfield and Deepfield Extension (BCN), 88–90, 98, 105–6; *see also* Tunnels, Coseley
Boats: day, 154; fly, 155–7, 178–9; iron, 154; 'Night and Sunday', 156; steam, 155, 179
Boatmen, 18, 142, 145, 148, 159
Bordesley Canal (Birmingham & Warwick Junction Canal), 112–13
Bough, John (engineer), 42–3, 163; relations with Pinkerton, 44
Boulton, Matthew, 14, 74, 77, 79, 89
Boulton & Watt, 77, 79–80, 144, 165
Brades, the, 98–9, 106
Bradley Hall Branch, 77, 86

Brewin, Thomas, 58, 60–1
Brickkiln Piece (Gas St Basin), 19, 23–4, 155
Bridges, swivel, replaced, 93
Bridgewater, Duke of, 53
Brindley, James, 12–14, 17–18, 23–5, 28, 74; death, 28
Broadwaters, 40, 75–6, 79
Broadwaters Extension Canal (BCN), 42–3, 75, 85–9
Broadwaters and Walsall Canal (BCN), 88–9
Broadwaters and Wolverhampton Canal (BCN), 88
Brown, John (contractor), 31
Bull (engineer), 160, 163
Buxton, William (engineman), 146
Byelaws: BCN, 158–9; Dudley Canal, 158; Wyrley Canal, 157–8

'Canal Mania', 87
Clerks, 17, 161
Clowes, William (engineer), 54
Coalowners, 18, 21–2, 40, 56–7, 66, 71–2, 75–6, 79–81, 84–8, 90, 101, 106–7, 124–5, 131, 140–3, 151, 174
Coal prices, 19–21, 26, 29, 52, 57, 65, 140–1
Coal trade: by BCN, 22, 139–43; by Dudley Canal, 56–7; by Wyrley Canal, 65
Collins, Joshua (boatman), 148
Coleshill Agreement, 40–2
Coventry Canal, 33, 39, 41, 45, 63, 135

Dadford, Thomas, 30, 35
Dallaway, Joseph, 17
Danks Branch (BCN), 111–12
Dartmouth, Earl of, 26, 53, 121

INDEX   201

Daw End Branch (Wyrley Canal), 112
'Deed of Compromise', 26
Digbeth Extension (BCN), 39
Digbeth Branch (BCN), 48
Downing, Francis, 124-5
'Drawbacks': on BCN, 174; on Dudley Canal, 58; on Wyrley Canal, 65
Dredging, 147-8; by machine, 76, 148
Dudley Canal, 29-38, 42, 47, 51, 77, 94-5, 108, 111; extension to Selly Oak, 51-61; junction with BCN, 32-4; lime trade on, 57-8; merger with BCN, 184-5; route, 31; proprietors, 124-5; and Stourbridge Canal, 30; traders assisted, 57; tramways, 56
Dudley, Earl of, 30-2, 34, 56-7, 59-60, 95, 124
Dudley and Finch (coalowners), 85
Dudley's, Lord, Canal (Lord Ward's Canal), 32-3

Engines, Pumping, *see* Pumping Engines
Enginemen, 146-7, 164
Exchequer Loan Commissioners, 101

Fereday, J. T. (ironmaster), 136
Finance: BCN, 89, 100-4, 126-39; (accounts), 130-1, 132-5; (debts), 131; (debentures), 103-4; Dudley Canal, 31, 36-7, 55-6, 58-9; (shares), 34-6; Wyrley Canal, 64-5; (shares), 63-4, 72-3
Firefighting in mines, 144
Foley, Edward, 88

Foley, Mrs Edward (coalowner), 87, 89
Foley, Thomas, 31
Freeth, John, 99-100, 116, 131, 161, 177
Friday Street (temporary terminus, BCN), 19, 24, 162

Galton, Samuel, 38-9, 78
Galton, Samuel, jnr, 93, 126
Galton, Samuel Tertius, 101, 120-22, 144
Galton Bridge, 84, 106
Garbett, Samuel, 11, 14, 18, 20, 22-4; dispute with Bentley, 20
Gauging stops, 105, 139
Gospel Oak Branch (BCN), 41, 77, 86
Gower Branch (BCN), 106
Grand Junction Canal, 53, 92, 131, 174, 175
Grand Trunk Canal, *see* Trent & Mersey Canal
Green, James (engineer), 30

Haines Branch (BCN), 106
Hawkes (mineowner): undermining canal, 75, 153
Haycock, John (steerer), 145
Hayhead Branch (Wyrley Canal), 63-4
Hellier, Shaw (coalowner), 59
Hood, Robert (engineer), 162, 165
Hordern, James, 66, 69, 125
Houghton, John, 45, 94, 97, 99, 161, 163

Icknield Port Loop (BCN), 91
Industrial development, 12, 104, 109-10
Ironmasters, 107, 135

'Island Line' (BCN), 98–101, 104, 106–9
Ison Arm (BCN), 84

James, William, 167
James Green embankment, 89
Jesson Arm (BCN), 84
Jessop, William, 35–6

Kettle, John, 14, 17

Labour force (BCN): clerical, 160–61; engineering, 161–2; manual, 163–4
Lawley, Sir Robert, MP, 52
Lee, T. Eyre, 101–2, 148; family influence, 120–1, 122
Lees, Abraham, 35
'Little Railway Mania', 172
Lloyd, Sampson, 11, 80, 128; family influence, 120–1
Locke, Joseph, 174
Locks: Ashted (BCN), 48; Black Delph (Dudley Canal), 31; Bradley Hall (BCN), 77; Curdworth (Fazeley Canal), 48; (extending opening times), 155–6; Farmer's Bridge (BCN), 44, 77, 81; (congestion at), 110–11, 114, 156–7, 175, 177; (and alternative routes), 72; (lighting), 156–7; Gospel Oak (BCN) (proposed), 77; Perry Bar (BCN), 112; Riders Green (BCN), 77, 86, 139; Smethwick (BCN), 17, 101, (duplicated) 83; Spon Lane (BCN), 77, 101; Tipton Green (BCN), 85; Toll End (BCN), 77, 151; Wolverhampton (BCN), 24, 28, 157 (bottom lock improved), 82–3; forty-foot lock proposed, 90

Locks, stop: BCN/Dudley, 33–4, 37–8, 108, 134–5; BCN/Worcester (Worcester Bar), 97; BCN/Wyrley, 62–3
Lock-keepers, 18, 162–4 (Tipton), 59
Loxdale, Thomas (coalowner), 87–8
Lyttleton, Sir Edward, 26

Maintenance, 144–53; contracts, 152–3; inspectors, 105, 164; workmen, 163–4
Making, George (contractor), 31
Manchester & Birmingham Junction Canal, 177
Meredith, William, 17, 29, 46, 158, 161
Mineowners, see Coalowners
Mines under Canal, 16, 75–6, 151–2
Mines Engines, see Pumping Engines
Monopoly by BCN, alleged, 21–2, 40, 140
Murdock, William, 146, 148

New Hall Ring, 22–4, 42

Ocker Hill Branch (BCN), 28, 75
Old Wednesbury Canal, 86
Oxford Canal, 33, 38, 40, 139, 174, 178

Parkes, Joseph, 111
Parliamentary intrigues (against Selly Oak Canal), 52–3
Pickfords (carriers), 159, 175–6, 179
Pilfering, 93, 142, 159–60
Pinkerton, John (contractor) and Bough, 44; and Broadwaters,

Pinkerton, John cont.
  42; and Dudley Canal, 35–6; and Fazeley Canal, 43–5; financial problems with BCN, 45; and Trent & Mersey Canal, 42–3
Pitt, William (engineer), 62
Pratt, Isaac, 35
Profits and dividends: BCN, 128–30; (use of), 13–15, 20–1; (effect of railways), 179–80; (excessive), 40; (limitation proposed), 15; Dudley Canal, 59; Staffs & Worcs Canal, 128
Proprietors: of BCN, 13, 120–1; of Dudley Canal, 124–5; of Wyrley Canal, 125–6
Pumping Engines: Ashted (BCN), 78–9, 146–7; Broadwaters (BCN), 79–80; Busseys Hollows (Dudley Canal), 33; Caponfield (BCN), 80–1, 117; costs, 78, 146; James Green (BCN) (proposed), 80; Ocker Hill (BCN), 75–8; Smethwick (BCN), 17, 75, 77; Spon Lane (BCN), 74–5, 77, 79; Titford (BCN), 117

Railways: attitude of BCN towards, 167–8, 172–4; Birmingham, Dudley and Wolverhampton, 172–3; Birmingham and Shrewsbury, 182–3; collieries to Birmingham (proposed), 167; competition with, 174–5, 177; co-operation with, 173–4; Dudley and Bescot, 182; Grand Junction, 172, 175, 182, 184; improvements caused by, 103, 107, 167, 177–8; Liverpool and Birmingham, 167–72; Liverpool & Manchester, 167; London & Birmingham, 172–5, 182; London & North Western, 184; Oxford, Worcester & Wolverhampton, 182; Stourbridge and Birmingham, 183; Wolverhampton and Birmingham, 107; Worcester and Wolverhampton, 172
Rates, parish, 137–9
Rennie, John, 78, 82, 85, 91–2, 94
Reservoirs: Birmingham Heath (BCN), 82; Cannock Heath (Wyrley Canal), 66, 77, 81, 117; Pensnett Chase (Dudley Canal), 31–2; Rotton Park (BCN), 81, 102–4, 117; Row Brook (BCN) (proposed), 82; Smethwick (BCN), 82, 117; Titford (BCN), 82; Walsall (BCN) (proposed), 81
Riders Green, 42
Ridgeacre Branch (BCN), 104
Roberts, Charles, 124
Rochdale Canal, 109, 173
Rushall Branch (BCN), 112, 114, 116

Sandy Turn (BCN) improvement at, 91–2
Selly Oak Branch (Dudley Canal), 51, 54–6; (parliamentary intrigues), 52–3
Severn, River, 12, 46
Sheasby, Thomas (contractor), 42, 44
Shirley, Hon Washington, 95
Sickness benefit, 165
Simcock, Samuel, 17–19, 24
Smeaton, John, 33, 74, 83, 87
Smethwick Cutting: first, 83–4; second, 99, 101–6, 148–9
Smethwick, new line to, 104
Snape, John (engineer), 33

Staffordshire & Worcestershire Canal, 13, 16, 18, 20, 24–5, 29, 30, 33, 46, 66, 82–3, 87–8, 92, 139, 147, 178, 182; junction with BCN, 24–8
Stoppages, 147–8
Stourbridge Canal, 29–30, 57–8; and Dudley Canal, 30, 57–8
Stratford-upon-Avon Canal, 48, 51, 57–8, 94–5, 111, 175, 177
Subsidence, 66, 75–6, 151–2
Superintendent of Works, 16, 161–2; connives at bad work, 44

Tame Valley Canal, 93, 111–16
Telford, Thomas, 69, 99, 101–2, 104–6, 167; achievements, 109; and contractors, 102; and maintenance, 105; reports on BCN, 99–100
Thomas, Robert, 116
Titford Branch (BCN), 107–9, 117
Tolls: BCN, 16, 29, 108, 131, 135–6, 175; (annual licensing), 135–6; (reductions refused), 131, 135, 174; (reductions begun), 175; credit, 136; Coventry and Warwick Canals' monopoly rates, 116, 175, 178; Dudley Canal, 30–1, 58; Selly Oak Canal, 54; Wyrley Canal, 62–3
Tolls, compensation: for Bilston subscribers, 41; BCN (from Dudley Canal), 32, 34, 108; (from Warwick Canal), 48, 94, 108; (from Worcester Canal), 94–5, 97, 111–12; (from Wyrley Canal), 63, 71; Staffs and Worcs Canal (from Birmingham and Liverpool Junction Canal), 178; Warwick and Birmingham Canal (from Stratford Canal), 50–1
Toll End Branch (BCN), 41, 85
Tonnage: checking, 136–7; effects of railways, 174–6, 180–2
Townshend (contractor), 106, 113
Trade: on BCN, 109, 116, 155, 157, 180–2; on Dudley Canal, 57–8
Tramways: on Dudley Canal, 56; on Wyrley Canal, 69
Trent & Mersey (Grand Trunk) Canal, 12, 21, 40–3, 139, 177
Trent, River, 12, 40
Trent, Tame and Anker Navigation, 40, 42
Tunnels, Coseley (BCN), 88, 98, 106–9; Dudley (Dudley Canal), 35–6, 37, 151; (byelaws), 59–60; (condition), 57, 60; (congestion in), 59; Gosty Hill (Dudley Canal), 54; (engine at), 60; Lappal (Dudley Canal), 54–5; (byelaws), 59–60, 158; (condition), 59, 60–1; (engine at), 61; Lodge Farm (Dudley Canal), 56; Netherton (BCN) (proposed), 52; Smethwick (BCN) (proposed), 17, 74; Wast Hill (Worcester Canal), 47

Vernon, Henry, 65–6, 125; dispute with Wyrley Canal, 66–70

Wages, 90, 142, 161–5
Walker, James (engineer), 112–13
Wall and Danks (coalowners): undermining canal, 75
Walsall Junction Canal, 70–2, 98, 116
Walsall Limeworks Branch (BCN) (proposed), 90–1

Ward's, Lord Canal (Lord Dudley's Canal), 32–3
Warwick & Birmingham Canal, 47–8, 77–8, 93–4, 108–9, 111–12, 135, 146–7, 152
Warwick & Napton Canal, 48–9, 174
Water losses, 144–5
Water supply: BCN, 74–82, 116–19; Dudley Canal, 30–3; and mills, 16; purchases, 77, 81; Warwick Canal, 146–7; Worcester Canal, 47, 95, 97; Wyrley Canal, 61
Watt, James, 26, 33, 77–9, 92–3, 102, 144
Weirs: raised by BCN, 37–8, 147; Wyrley to flow to BCN, 61–2
Wharfingers, 18, 162
Wharves: BCN, 22, 108–9, 155; Dudley Canal, 58
Whitby, Mrs (coalowner), 87, 89
Whitmore and Norton (engineers), 90
Whitworth, Robert (engineer), 16, 55

Wildgoose, John (surveyor), 35
Wilkinson, John, 79, 90, 104, 145
Wilkinson, Joseph, 17
Winson Green and Soho branch (BCN) (proposed), 86, 88
Wood (coalowner): undermining canal, 75
Wood Green Branch (BCN) (proposed), 113, 116
Worcester & Birmingham Canal, 46–7, 51, 56–8, 80, 92, 94–5, 131
Worcester Basin and Camp Hill, Canal (proposed), 111
Worcester Bar, 47, 93–7
Worcester and Stourbridge Canal (proposed), 46
Work force, *see* Labour Supply
Wyrley & Essington Canal, 61–73; dispute with Vernon, 66–70; extension, 63; finance, 63–4; merger with BCN, 70–3; proprietors, 125–6; shares, 63–4; tramways, 69